Coffee Cookbook

The perfect Coffee Lover's Guide to Quickly Master Barista Skills and WOW friends and family with Easy and Delicious Homemade Coffee-Based Recipes. No-Fuss, Just Flavor!"

Arabella Bennet

Copyright

TABLE OF CONTENTS

🎁 HERE IS YOUR FREE GIFT!

👉 SCAN HERE TO DOWNLOAD IT

INTRODUCTION

As a coffee expert, I've had the unique privilege of immersing myself in the rich tapestry of coffee culture that spans the globe. My journey with coffee has been one of discovery, learning, and, above all, a deep appreciation for this remarkable beverage that so many of us hold dear.

On this personal note, I want to share with you the essence of my experiences and the profound impact coffee has had on my life and the lives of countless others. Coffee is more than just a drink, it's a universal language that transcends borders and unites people from all walks of life. From the sun-drenched plantations of Ethiopia, where the Arabica bean first took root, to the bustling cafes of Rome that pulse with the energy of expertly crafted espressos, coffee tells a story of human connection, innovation, and passion. My love affair with coffee began in my youth, not with a sip, but with a scent. The aroma of freshly ground coffee beans wafting through my family's kitchen was the first thread of a bond that would weave its way through every aspect of my life. As I grew older, I sought to understand the source of this enchanting elixir. I traveled to remote villages where coffee is not merely a crop, but a cherished heritage passed down through generations who respect and revere the land that sustains their livelihood.

Through my travels, I've witnessed the meticulous care of coffee farmers who rise with the dawn, tending to their crops with a dedication that borders on the sacred. I've sat with them, hands stained with soil, as they shared their stories and their dreams, revealing a world where coffee is the lifeblood of communities. In the bustling cities, I've observed the artistry of baristas who command their espresso machines with the precision of a conductor, each cup a symphony of flavor and craftsmanship.

I've engaged in spirited debates with fellow aficionados about the nuances of roast profiles and the virtues of different brewing methods. And in these moments, I've seen the power of coffee to ignite creativity, conversation, and camaraderie.

But my relationship with coffee is not just one of romance; it is also one of reverence for its complexity and respect for its impact. Coffee is a teacher, offering lessons in sustainability, health, and the importance of mindful consumption. It has taught me that every choice we make, from the beans we select to the way we brew, has a ripple effect that touches farmers, communities, and ecosystems around the world. As we delve into the pages of this cookbook, I invite you to join me on a journey that is not just about savoring the perfect cup, but about understanding the intricate web of stories, people, and processes that make it possible. We'll explore the health benefits that make coffee a surprising ally in our quest for wellness, and we'll confront the challenges that remind us to drink responsibly and ethically.

This book is a tribute to coffee and to the millions of individuals who cultivate, craft, and cherish it every day. It is a collection of knowledge, experiences, and recipes that I have gathered over a lifetime of exploration. Whether you're a seasoned coffee lover or new to the wonders of this beloved brew, I hope to inspire you with a deeper appreciation for the art and science of coffee. So, as you turn these pages, imagine the journey of the humble coffee bean—from the soil to your cup—and remember that each sip is a testament to the hands that have nurtured it. Together, let's celebrate the rich, bold, and diverse world of coffee, and may your journey be as fulfilling and flavored as the drink we all adore.

The Essence of Coffee: Understanding Your Brew Coffee, a beverage as complex as it is captivating, invites us to explore its multifaceted nature. Each cup offers a window into a world of nuanced flavors and aromas, a testament to the journey from bean to brew. In this section, we delve into the essence of coffee, unraveling the threads that compose the rich tapestry of your daily cup. At its core, coffee is an alchemy of science and art. The humble coffee bean, the seed of the coffee cherry, carries within it the potential for a myriad of tastes and experiences.

The species of the coffee plant, primarily Arabica and Robusta, set the stage for the flavor profile. Arabica, with its delicate, nuanced notes, hails from the highlands of Ethiopia, requiring precise conditions to flourish. Robusta, bolder and more assertive, thrives in diverse climates, offering a heartier bean with a punch of caffeine. The journey from green bean to your cup is marked by the transformative process of roasting. Roasting levels, from light to dark, dictate the color, flavor, and acidity of the bean. Light roasts, kissed by heat just long enough to awaken their bright, acidic notes, preserve the bean's original character. Dark roasts, on the other hand, linger in the heat, developing a robust, bitter profile with a full body that lingers on the palate.

The grind of the bean is the next critical step in crafting your brew. The granularity, from coarse to fine, must be matched to the brewing method to extract the coffee's soul. A coarse grind, perfect for a French press, allows for a slower extraction, yielding a full-flavored cup. A fine grind, ideal for espresso, creates a concentrated shot with a creamy body and a rich crema. Water, the unsung hero of the coffee world, plays a pivotal role in the brewing process. Its temperature and quality can elevate or diminish the coffee's essence.

The right water temperature extracts the optimal flavor, while the purity of the water ensures that no external flavors taint the coffee's profile. Understanding your brew is also about recognizing the influence of geography and culture. Coffee is a global affair, with each region imparting its signature to the beans.

The volcanic soils of Central America, the tropical climates of Africa, and the lush landscapes of South America all contribute to the diversity of flavors in your cup. However, the essence of coffee is not solely in its physical attributes. It's in the morning ritual, the comforting warmth of the mug between your hands. It's in the pause during a busy day, a moment of reflection during chaos. Coffee is a companion for conversation, a catalyst for creativity, and a bridge between cultures. As we explore the essence of coffee, we embark on a sensory journey. We learn to savor the subtleties of each sip, to appreciate the craftsmanship behind the brew, and to understand the global narrative interwoven with each bean. Coffee is not just a drink; it's an experience, a philosophy, a way of life. Embrace the journey and let the essence of coffee guide you to a deeper appreciation of this extraordinary beverage.

How to Navigate This Cookbook for the Best Coffee Experience Navigating a cookbook can be as much an adventure as exploring a new city. With the "Coffee CookBook"," you're not just flipping through pages of recipes; you're embarking on a journey through the world of coffee. This section will serve as your compass, guiding you on how to make the most of this book for the ultimate coffee experience.

First, consider this cookbook your coffee atlas. Each chapter is a new destination, offering insights into different aspects of coffee culture and preparation. Each recipe in the book is more than a set of instructions; it's a story and an experience. Take the time to read the introductions to the recipes, where you'll find anecdotes, tips, and the history behind each brew. These narratives will enrich your brewing process and deepen your appreciation for the cup in your hand.

 Remember, this cookbook is not meant to be read linearly. Feel free to jump between chapters as you please. As you navigate through the "Coffee CookBook" keep in mind that coffee is personal. Use this book to experiment and find what suits your taste best. The measurements and methods provided are starting points; don't be afraid to adjust them to your liking. Coffee is as much about personal preference as it is about technique.

Lastly, engage with the book. Make notes in the margins of your favorite recipes, mark pages with sticky notes, and document your coffee experiments. This cookbook should be a living document, one that grows with you as you continue to explore the vast and vibrant world of coffee. In essence, " Cofee CookBook " is more than a collection of recipes, it's a guide to discovering the joy and complexity of coffee. Use it to navigate your way to the perfect cup, explore new horizons in your coffee journey, and savor each moment along the way. Welcome to the best coffee experience of your life.

THE FUNDAMENTALS OF COFFEE

2.1 Quick Coffee Basics: Beans, Roasts, and Grinds

At the heart of the coffee experience lies the humble coffee bean, not merely a seed but a vessel of potential flavors that shape your coffee's character. There are two primary species: Arabica and Robusta, each distinct in its essence. Arabica, the more esteemed, is celebrated for its smooth, often intricate flavor profiles, boasting a sweeter, gentler taste with hints ranging from sugar and fruit to more exotic wine or floral notes. With less caffeine, Arabica beans are less bitter, yet their cultivation demands specific conditions, higher altitudes and cooler climates, as found in Ethiopia and Latin America. This sensitivity to the environment renders Arabica beans typically more costly.

Conversely, Robusta beans, true to their name, are hardier. They possess a potent, more austere taste with grain-like overtones and a nutty aftertaste. Higher in caffeine, these beans not only impart a more bitter flavor but also bestow greater resilience against pests and diseases. They thrive in lower altitudes and warmer climes, common in parts of Africa and Southeast Asia. Robusta finds favor in espresso blends for its rich crema and robust flavor and is generally more affordable than Arabica.

Roasts: Crafting the Character

The transformation of coffee beans from raw, green to aromatic and flavorful is achieved through roasting, a process of applying heat that ignites a series of chemical reactions. Light roasts, light brown in color, are halted at the first crack, a moment when beans expand and crack audibly. These roasts, devoid of oil on the bean surface, are noted for their high acidity and preserve much of the bean's origin-specific flavors, which may include fruity or floral notes. Medium roasts, darker in hue, offer a harmonious balance of flavor, aroma, and acidity, often favored in the United States and known as American roast. They reveal the beans' inherent sweetness while maintaining some original flavors. Dark roasts, dark brown or near black with an oily surface, are marked by a pronounced bitterness, with flavors described as smoky or chocolatey. In these, the bean's original flavors are largely eclipsed by those developed in the roast, making them ideal for strong coffee and espresso.

Grinds: The Final Adjustment

The grind size of coffee beans is pivotal in brewing, influencing the extraction rate of flavors. The choice of grind should align with the brewing method for optimal flavor. Coarse grinds, akin to sea salt, suit methods like French press or cold brew, where extended contact between water and coffee occurs. A coarse grind wards off over-extraction and resultant bitterness. Medium grinds, comparable to sand, are versatile, fitting for drip coffee makers and pour-over brewers. This grind size allows for a balanced extraction. Fine grinds, smooth like sugar or salt, are perfect for espresso machines, enabling quick and intense extraction, essential for a rich, full-bodied espresso. Adjusting grind size can refine the brew to your preference: a finer grind for a more extracted, flavorful cup if the coffee is too weak or sour; a coarser grind for a smoother taste if the coffee is overly strong or bitter.

2.2 Essential Equipment: Simplifying Your Coffee Toolkit

Embarking on home coffee brewing, whether as an aficionado or a novice, necessitates the right equipment to achieve the ideal cup. Following our exploration of beans, roasts, and grinds in "Part I: The Fundamentals of Coffee," we now delve into the essential apparatus needed to unify these elements. The coffee maker is central, with various types influencing the brew's flavor profile. Drip Coffee Makers, prevalent for their convenience, drip hot water over coffee grounds, filtering into a carafe. French Presses, known for rich, full-bodied coffee, steep grounds in hot water, separated by a plunger. Espresso Machines, for concentrated coffee, employ high pressure to push water through finely-ground coffee. Pour-Over Gear offers control over brewing time and temperature, yielding clean, nuanced flavors. AeroPress, a newer method, is versatile and portable, capable of producing different coffee styles.

Grinders are essential for freshness. Freshly ground coffee maximizes flavor, whereas pre-ground can lose nuances. Blade Grinders, more affordable, chop beans with a spinning blade but may yield uneven grinds affecting taste. Burr Grinders ensure consistent grind size, crucial for flavor extraction, and can be adjusted for various brewing methods.

Scales and measuring tools bring precision to coffee making. A digital scale ensures exact coffee and water quantities for consistent strength and flavor, while a timer aids in brewing, particularly for pour-over and French press methods. Kettles, especially important for pour-over and French press, vary. Gooseneck kettles provide control over pour speed and direction, crucial for even coffee ground saturation. Temperature control kettles allow heating water to specific temperatures ideal for the coffee being brewed.

Maintaining equipment is vital for its longevity and your coffee's taste. This includes descaling solutions for machines, brush sets for grinders and safe cleaning agents for coffee makers.

2.3 The Art of the Perfect Brew: Techniques and Tips

Mastering coffee brewing, a pursuit of the perfect cup tailored to individual taste, follows an understanding of beans and equipment. This section imparts techniques and tips for refining your brewing process across various methods, from simple drip coffee makers to more hands-on approaches like pour-over or French press. Understanding extraction, the process of drawing flavors from coffee grounds, is key. The goal is a balanced extraction, capturing desirable flavors without over-extracting bitter compounds. Factors influencing this include grind size, affecting extraction rate; water temperature, ideally between 195°F to 205°F (90°C to 96°C); and brew time, varying with grind size and method.

The coffee-to-water ratio also impacts brew strength and flavor, commonly starting at 1:16 (one part coffee to sixteen parts water), adjustable to taste.

Each brewing method has its techniques. Drip Coffee requires even saturation of grounds, a medium grind, and the correct water temperature. French Press benefits from a coarse grind and a four-minute steep before plunging. Espresso demands a fine grind and even tamping for uniform water passage. Pour-Over involves controlling the pour, starting with a small amount of water to "bloom" the coffee, followed by a slow, spiral pour. AeroPress allows experimentation with grind size and pressure.

Consistency tips include using fresh water, regular cleaning of equipment, precise measurements, and keeping a brewing journal. Troubleshooting common issues like bitter (over-extraction) or sour (under-extraction) flavors, weak or strong coffee, involves adjusting grind size, brew time, or water temperature.

This section aims to empower you with knowledge to enhance your brewing skills, ensuring a delicious, consistent cup of coffee.

QUICK AND EASY COFFEE RECIPES

3.1 Morning Kickstart to Energize Your Day

1 CLASSIC ESPRESSO SHOT

An essential for coffee enthusiasts, the classic espresso is a concentrated, full-flavored coffee that is the foundation of many popular coffee drinks. Perfecting the art of espresso making can be a rewarding experience, offering a deep appreciation for the subtleties of coffee flavor.

Ingredients:
» 1 tablespoons of fine espresso ground coffee
» Fresh, cold water

Preparation Time:
2 minutes

Directions:
1. Warm Up Your Espresso Machine: Start turning on your espresso machine to heat it. Ensure the portafilter is locked in to warm up as well.
2. Grind the Coffee: Grind your coffee beans to a fine espresso grind. The grind should be fine but not so powdery that it impedes water flow.
3. Measure the Coffee: Measure out 1.25 oz of the ground coffee for a double shot.
4. Prepare the Portafilter: Remove the portafilter from the machine, empty any old grounds, and wipe it clean. Add the freshly ground coffee to the portafilter.
5. Tamp the Coffee: Use a tamper to press the coffee down evenly with firm pressure. The surface should be smooth and level.
6. Brew the Espresso: Return the portafilter to the machine and start the brew immediately. A good espresso should take about 25-30 seconds to brew.
7. Serve: Once the espresso is brewed, it should have a thick, golden crema on top. Serve immediately for the best taste.

2 CARAMEL MACCHIATO

A delightful coffee beverage, known for its layers of sweet caramel, rich espresso, and smooth steamed milk. It's a popular choice for those who enjoy a balance of sweetness with their coffee.

Ingredients:
- » 1 cup of Milk
- » 1 shot of Espresso
- » 2 tablespoons of Vanilla syrup
- » 2 tablespoons of Caramel sauce: plus extra for drizzling
- » Ice (optional, for an iced version)

Preparation Time:
5 minutes

Directions:
1. Steam Milk: Start by steaming the milk until it's hot and frothy. If you don't have a steamer, you can heat the milk in the microwave or on the stove and then whisk it vigorously or use a milk frother.
2. Prepare Espresso: Brew one shot of espresso using an espresso machine or a strong coffee alternative like a Moka pot or an Aeropress.
3. Add Vanilla Syrup: In a large cup, pour the vanilla syrup.
4. Pour Milk: Add the steamed milk to the cup with the vanilla syrup, holding back the foam with a spoon to let the milk flow in first.
5. Add Espresso: Gently pour the espresso shot over the milk.
6. Drizzle with Caramel: Drizzle caramel sauce over the top in a circular motion or a crisscross pattern.
7. Serve: If desired, spoon the reserved foam on top and add an extra drizzle of caramel sauce for a decorative touch. For an iced version, add ice to the cup before adding milk and espresso.

3 SPICED ORANGE COFFEE

A warm, aromatic blend that combines the richness of coffee with the zesty freshness of orange and the subtle warmth of spices. This recipe is perfect for those looking for a unique twist on their regular coffee routine.

Ingredients:
- » 2 tablespoons of Freshly ground coffee beans
- » 1 cup of Water
- » 1 teaspoon of Orange zest
- » 1 stick of Cinnamon
- » 2 Cloves
- » 1 Star anise
- » Honey or sugar to taste (optional)
- » Whipped cream for garnish (optional)
- » Orange slice for garnish (optional)

Preparation Time:
7 minutes

Directions:
1. Heat Water: In a small saucepan, bring the water to a boil.
2. Add Spices: Once the water is boiling, add the cinnamon stick, cloves, star anise, and orange zest. Reduce the heat and let it simmer for 3-5 minutes to infuse the flavors.
3. Brew Coffee: Meanwhile, brew your coffee using your preferred method. A French press or pour-over works well for this.
4. Combine: Strain the spiced water into the brewed coffee. Stir well.
5. Sweeten: Add honey or sugar to taste, if desired.
6. Serve: Pour the spiced coffee into a mug. If you like, top with a dollop of whipped cream and garnish with an orange slice.
7. Enjoy: Savor the unique combination of coffee, citrus, and spices.

4 PEPPERMINT MOCHA

A festive and comforting beverage, combining the rich flavors of chocolate and coffee with a refreshing hint of peppermint. It's a holiday favorite, perfect for chilly weather and cozy gatherings.

Ingredients:
» 1 shot of freshly brewed espresso
» 1 cup of Milk (whole or your choice)
» 2 tablespoons of Chocolate syrup
» ¼ teaspoon of Peppermint extract
» Whipped cream (optional)
» Crushed peppermint candy or peppermint stick (optional for garnish)
» Cocoa powder or chocolate shavings (optional for garnish)

Preparation Time:
12 minutes

Directions:
1. Heat Milk: Start by heating the milk in a saucepan over medium heat until hot but not boiling. Alternatively, you can heat it in the microwave.
2. Add Chocolate Syrup: Add the chocolate syrup to the milk, whisking until fully blended.
3. Infuse Peppermint Flavor: Stir in the peppermint extract into the chocolate milk mixture. Be careful with the amount, as peppermint extract is quite strong.
4. Brew Espresso: Brew a shot of espresso or strong coffee. If you're using a coffee maker, opt for a dark roast for a richer flavor.
5. Combine: Pour the espresso into a large cup. Add the peppermint-chocolate milk mixture over the coffee.
6. Add Whipped Cream: If desired, top your peppermint mocha with a generous dollop of whipped cream.
7. Garnish: Sprinkle crushed peppermint candy, a peppermint stick, cocoa powder, or chocolate shavings on top for an extra festive touch.
8. Serve the peppermint mocha immediately. Enjoy the warm, minty, chocolatey goodness, perfect for holiday mornings or as a delightful treat on a cold evening.

5 ANTIOXIDANT BERRY BLAST COFFEE SMOOTHIE

This Antioxidant Berry Blast Coffee Smoothie is a nutritious and energizing start to your day, blending the rich taste of coffee with the natural sweetness and health benefits of various berries. It's perfect for those mornings when you need an extra boost.

Ingredients:

» 1 cup of Chilled brewed coffee
» 1 cup of Frozen mixed berries (such as blueberries, strawberries)
» 1 ripe of raspberries or Banana
» ½ cup of Greek yogurt or plant-based yogurt
» 1 tablespoon of Honey or maple syrup: (optional, depending on desired sweetness)
» 1 tablespoon of Ground flaxseed or chia seeds
» ½ cup of Ice cubes
» ½ cup of Almond milk or milk of choice (adjust according to desired consistency)

Preparation Time:
12 minutes

Directions:

1. Prepare Coffee: Brew your coffee and allow it to chill in the refrigerator. You can do this the night before to save time in the morning.
2. Combine Ingredients: In a blender, add the chilled coffee, frozen mixed berries, ripe banana, yogurt, honey or maple syrup (if using), ground flaxseed or chia seeds, and ice cubes.
3. Blend: Blend on high speed until all the ingredients are thoroughly combined and the mixture is smooth. If the smoothie is too thick, you can add more almond milk or regular milk to reach your preferred consistency.
4. Taste and Adjust: Taste the smoothie and adjust the sweetness if necessary. If you prefer a thinner consistency, add a little more milk or coffee.
5. Serve: Pour the smoothie into a glass and serve immediately.

3.2 Midday Revival to Beat the Afternoon Slump

6 GINGER SNAP LATTE

The Ginger Snap Latte is a delightful beverage that encapsulates the essence of ginger snap cookies in a warm, comforting coffee drink. Its blend of spices and sweetness is perfect for those crisp mornings or cozy afternoons.

Ingredients:
- » 2 shots of freshly brewed espresso or strong coffee
- » 1 ½ cups milk (whole or your choice)
- » ½ teaspoon of ground ginger
- » ½ teaspoon of ground cinnamon
- » A pinch of ground nutmeg
- » 1 tablespoon of molasses
- » 1 tablespoon of brown sugar (can adjust based on sweetness preference)
- » Whipped cream (optional for topping)
- » Ginger snap cookies (crumbled, optional for garnish)
- » Additional cinnamon or nutmeg (optional for garnish)

Preparation Time:
10 minutes

Directions:
1. Spice Infusion: In a small saucepan, combine milk, ground ginger, cinnamon, nutmeg, molasses, and brown sugar. Heat over medium heat, whisking constantly to ensure the spices and sweeteners are well incorporated and the milk doesn't scald. Heat until the mixture is hot but not boiling.
2. Brew Espresso: While the milk mixture is heating, brew your espresso or strong coffee. Opt for a rich, dark roast to complement the bold spice flavors if using a coffee maker.
3. Foam the Milk: Once the milk mixture is hot, use a frother to foam the milk to your desired consistency. If you don't have a frother, you can whisk vigorously by hand or use a blender, being careful with the hot liquid.
4. Assemble the Latte: Pour the brewed espresso or coffee into a large mug. Gently add the spiced milk mixture. For a layered effect, pour the milk slowly or use the back of a spoon to guide it.
5. Add Toppings: If desired, top with whipped cream. Sprinkle crumbled ginger snap cookies, and a pinch of cinnamon or nutmeg for garnish.
6. Serve your Ginger Snap Latte warm, stirring gently before sipping to blend the flavors.

7 CARDAMOM COFFEE SHAKE

The Cardamom Coffee Shake is a delightful blend of aromatic cardamom, rich coffee, and creamy sweetness. It's an excellent choice for those who love a spiced twist to their coffee, offering a refreshing and energizing experience.

Ingredients:

» 1 cup of strongly brewed coffee, cooled
» 2 scoops of vanilla ice cream
» ½ cup milk (whole or your choice)
» ½ teaspoon ground cardamom
» 1 cup of ice cubes
» Whipped cream (optional, for topping)
» Ground cinnamon or additional cardamom (optional, for garnish)

Preparation Time:
12 minutes

Directions:
1. Prepare Coffee: Brew a strong cup of coffee and allow it to cool. You can place it in the refrigerator to speed up the cooling process.
2. Blend Ingredients: In a blender, combine the cooled coffee, vanilla ice cream, milk, ground cardamom, and ice cubes. Blend until smooth and creamy.
3. Check Consistency: If the shake is too thick, you can add a little more milk to reach your desired consistency. If it's too thin, add a bit more ice cream or ice cubes and blend again.
4. Serve: Pour the cardamom coffee shake into a tall glass. If desired, top with a dollop of whipped cream.
5. Garnish: Sprinkle a pinch of ground cinnamon or cardamom on top of the whipped cream for an extra burst of flavor and an appealing look.
6. Enjoy: Serve immediately and enjoy the rich, aromatic flavors of this unique coffee shake.

8 HONEY ALMOND LATTE

The Honey Almond Latte is a sweet and nutty coffee drink, combining the richness of espresso with the natural sweetness of honey and the distinct flavor of almond. It's a comforting beverage, perfect for those who enjoy a hint of sweetness and nuttiness in their coffee.

Ingredients:

» 1 shot of espresso or strong brewed coffee
» 1 cup of almond milk
» 1 tablespoon honey (adjust to taste)
» ¼ teaspoon almond extract
» A pinch of cinnamon powder (for garnish)
» Sliced almonds (optional, for garnish)

Preparation Time:
10 minutes

Directions:

1. Brew Espresso/Coffee: Start by brewing a shot of espresso or a strong coffee. If you're using a coffee maker, choose a dark roast for a richer flavor.
2. Warm Almond Milk: In a saucepan, gently heat the almond milk over medium heat. Be careful not to boil it; you want it hot and steamy.
3. Infuse with Honey and Almond Extract: Once the almond milk is hot, remove it from the heat and stir in the honey and almond extract. Mix well until the honey is fully dissolved.
4. Froth the Milk: If you have a milk frother, froth the honey-almond milk mixture to your desired level of foam. If you don't have a frother, you can whisk it vigorously or use a blender, being cautious with the hot liquid.
5. Combine: Pour the freshly brewed espresso or coffee into a large mug. Gently add the frothed honey almond milk.
6. Garnish: Sprinkle a pinch of cinnamon powder on top for added flavor and aroma. You can also garnish with a few sliced almonds for a crunchy texture and visual appeal.
7. Serve the Honey Almond Latte immediately, stirring gently before sipping to blend the flavors.

9 COCONUT CREAM COLD BREW

The Coconut Cream Cold Brew is a lush and tropical twist on traditional cold brew coffee. It combines the smooth, rich taste of cold brew with the creamy, sweet flavor of coconut, making it a perfect refreshment for warm days or when you're looking for an indulgent coffee treat.

Ingredients:

» 2 cups of cold brew coffee
» ½ cup of coconut cream
» 2 tablespoons simple syrup or sweetener of choice (adjust to taste)
» ½ teaspoon of vanilla extract
» Ice cubes
» Toasted coconut flakes (optional, for garnish)

Preparation Time:
9 minutes
(excluding time to prepare cold brew)

Directions:

1. Prepare Cold Brew: If making your cold brew, do this in advance. Steep coarsely ground coffee in cold water for 12-24 hours, then strain. Store the cold brew in the refrigerator until ready to use.
2. Sweeten Coconut Cream: In a small bowl, combine the coconut cream, simple syrup (or your chosen sweetener), and vanilla extract. Stir well until the mixture is smooth and the sweetener is fully dissolved.
3. Assemble the Drink: Fill glasses with ice cubes. Pour the cold brew coffee over the ice, leaving some room at the top for the coconut cream.
4. Add Coconut Cream: Gently pour the sweetened coconut cream over the cold brew. It will create a beautiful layer on top of the coffee.
5. Garnish: If desired, sprinkle toasted coconut flakes on top for a crunchy texture and enhanced flavor.
6. Serve: Stir the Coconut Cream Cold Brew gently before drinking to mix the flavors or enjoy the layered taste with each sip.

10 MATCHA COFFEE FUSION

The Matcha Coffee Fusion is an innovative drink that combines the earthy depth of matcha green tea with the robust intensity of coffee. This fusion creates a unique beverage that's both energizing and full of flavor, perfect for those who love both coffee and tea.

Ingredients:

» ½ cup of strongly brewed coffee or strong coffee
» 1 teaspoon of matcha green tea powder
» ¼ cup of hot water
» ½ cup of milk (whole, almond, soy, or oat)
» 1 tablespoon of honey or sweetener of choice (optional)
» Ice cubes (for iced version)
» Whipped cream (optional, for garnish)

Preparation Time:
10 minutes

Directions:

1. Prepare Matcha: Sift the matcha powder into a small bowl to remove any lumps. Add the hot water and whisk vigorously in a zigzag motion until the matcha is fully dissolved and a light froth forms on top. A traditional bamboo whisk (chasen) works best for this.
2. Brew Coffee: Brew a strong half cup of coffee using your preferred method. Allow it to cool slightly if you're making a hot drink, or chill in the refrigerator if you're making an iced version.
3. Combine Matcha and Coffee: In a large cup or glass, combine the matcha mixture with the brewed coffee. Stir well to ensure they're fully mixed.
4. Heat or Froth Milk: If making a hot drink, heat the milk without boiling it and froth it if possible. For an iced drink, you can skip the frothing step.
5. Add Milk: Pour the milk into the matcha-coffee mixture. For an iced version, first, fill the glass with ice cubes before adding the milk.
6. Sweeten: Add honey or your preferred sweetener, adjusting to taste.
7. Garnish (Optional): Top with whipped cream if desired for an extra indulgent touch.
8. Serve immediately, enjoying the unique combination of matcha and coffee flavors.

11 CLASSIC AFFOGATO

The Classic Affogato is a simple yet luxurious Italian dessert that elegantly combines the rich taste of espresso with the creamy sweetness of ice cream. This dessert is both easy to prepare and delightful to savor, making it a perfect treat for any occasion.

Ingredients:

» 2 shots of freshly brewed espresso or strong coffee
» 2 scoops vanilla ice cream
» Dark chocolate shavings (optional, for garnish)
» Amaretto or coffee liqueur (optional, for an adult version)

Preparation Time:
5 minutes

Directions:

1. Prepare Espresso: Brew two shots of fresh espresso. If you don't have an espresso machine, you can use a strong brewed coffee as an alternative, though espresso is preferred for its intensity and flavor.
2. Scoop Ice Cream: Place one scoop of vanilla gelato or ice cream into each serving glass or bowl. Ideally, use a small, chilled glass or cup to serve.
3. Pour Espresso: Immediately pour a shot of hot espresso over each scoop of gelato or ice cream. The heat of the espresso will start to melt the gelato, creating a delicious creamy and coffee-infused mixture.
4. Add Optional Ingredients: If you're using dark chocolate shavings, sprinkle them on top for added texture and a hint of chocolate flavor. For an adult twist, you can add a splash of Amaretto or coffee liqueur.
5. Serve the affogato immediately after preparation. Provide a spoon for guests to enjoy the combination of warm espresso and cold, melting gelato.

12 CHOCOLATE RASPBERRY MOCHA

The Chocolate Raspberry Mocha is a decadent coffee drink that combines the rich flavors of chocolate and raspberry with the robust taste of coffee. This delightful beverage is perfect for those who love a fruity twist on their mocha.

Ingredients:

» 1 shot of freshly brewed espresso or strong coffee
» 1 cup of milk (whole, almond, or soy)
» 2 tablespoons of chocolate syrup
» 2 tablespoons of raspberry syrup
» Whipped cream (optional, for topping)
» Fresh raspberries (optional, for garnish)
» Chocolate shavings or cocoa powder (optional, for garnish)

Preparation Time:
10 minutes

Directions:

1. Brew Espresso/Coffee: Start by brewing a shot of espresso or strong coffee. If using a coffee maker, opt for a dark roast to get a rich flavor.
2. Heat Milk: In a saucepan or using a microwave, heat the milk until it's hot but not boiling. You can also froth the milk if you have a frother, for a creamier texture.
3. Mix in Syrups: Add the chocolate syrup and raspberry syrup to the milk. Stir well to ensure they are fully combined.
4. Combine with Coffee: Pour the freshly brewed espresso or coffee into a large mug. Add the flavored milk mixture to the coffee.
5. Top with Whipped Cream: If desired, top your Chocolate Raspberry Mocha with a generous amount of whipped cream.
6. Garnish: Garnish with fresh raspberries and chocolate shavings or a dusting of cocoa powder for an extra touch of elegance and flavor.
7. Serve the mocha immediately, stirring gently before sipping to blend all the flavors.

13 TOASTED MARSHMALLOW LATTE

The Toasted Marshmallow Latte is a cozy and indulgent coffee drink that captures the essence of a campfire treat. It combines the rich, comforting flavors of coffee and toasted marshmallows, making it a perfect choice for those chilly days or whenever you're in the mood for something sweet and soothing.

Ingredients:
» 2 shots of freshly brewed espresso or strong coffee
» 1 cup of milk (whole, almond, soy, or oat)
» 2 tablespoons of marshmallow syrup
» ½ teaspoonof vanilla extract
» 4-5 Marshmallows (for topping)
» Chocolate shavings or cocoa powder (optional, for garnish)
» Graham cracker crumbs (optional, for garnish)

Preparation Time:
12 minutes

Directions:
1. Brew Espresso/Coffee: Begin by brewing two shots of espresso or strong coffee. If you're using a coffee maker, choose a rich, bold roast to complement the sweetness of the marshmallows.
2. Heat and Froth Milk: In a saucepan or using a microwave, heat the milk until it's hot but not boiling. Froth the milk using a frother, whisk, or blender to create a creamy texture.
3. Flavor the Milk: Stir the marshmallow syrup and vanilla extract into the heated milk. Mix well to ensure the flavors are evenly distributed.
4. Combine with Coffee: Pour the freshly brewed espresso or coffee into a large mug. Add the flavored milk mixture over the coffee.
5. Toast Marshmallows: Place the marshmallows on a baking sheet and use a kitchen torch to toast them until golden brown. Alternatively, you can broil them in the oven, watching closely to prevent burning.
6. Top with Marshmallows: Carefully place the toasted marshmallows on top of the latte.
7. Add Garnishes: Sprinkle chocolate shavings or cocoa powder for a chocolatey touch, and graham cracker crumbs for that authentic s'mores flavor (both optional).
8. Serve the Toasted Marshmallow Latte immediately, offering a spoon to enjoy the gooey marshmallows.

14 TIRAMISU CAPPUCCINO

The Tiramisu Cappuccino is an exquisite coffee drink inspired by the classic Italian dessert. It blends the rich flavors of a traditional cappuccino with the sweet, creamy taste of tiramisu, making it a luxurious treat for coffee and dessert lovers alike.

Ingredients:

» 1 shot of freshly brewed espresso
» ¾ cup of milk (whole or your choice)
» 1 tablespoonof mascarpone cheese
» 1 teaspoon of cocoa powder, plus extra for dusting
» 1 teaspoon of sugar or sweetener of choice (adjust to taste)
» ¼ teaspoon of vanilla extract
» Ladyfinger biscuit (optional, for garnish)
» Grated dark chocolate (optional, for garnish)

Preparation Time:
10 minutes

Directions:

1. Brew Espresso: Begin by brewing a shot of espresso. A rich, dark roast coffee is preferred to mimic the robust flavor of traditional tiramisu.
2. Heat and Froth Milk: In a saucepan or using a microwave, heat the milk until it's hot but not boiling. Froth the milk using a milk frother, whisk, or blender to create a creamy texture.
3. Mix Mascarpone Mixture: In a small bowl, blend the mascarpone cheese, 1 teaspoon of cocoa powder, sugar, and vanilla extract. Mix until smooth and creamy.
4. Combine Mascarpone with Espresso: Pour the freshly brewed espresso into a large mug. Add the mascarpone mixture to the espresso and stir well to combine.
5. Add Frothed Milk: Gently pour the frothed milk into the mug, spooning the foam on top to create a classic cappuccino look.
6. Garnish: Dust the top with additional cocoa powder and grated dark chocolate for an authentic tiramisu flavor. Optionally, place a ladyfinger biscuit on the side of the cup for garnish.
7. Serve the Tiramisu Cappuccino immediately, enjoying the rich and creamy flavors reminiscent of the beloved Italian dessert.

15 NUTTY IRISHMAN COFFEE

The Nutty Irishman Coffee is a rich and indulgent beverage that combines the warm flavors of coffee with Irish cream and hazelnut liqueur. This delightful drink is perfect for those special occasions when you're in the mood for something sweet, creamy, and slightly boozy.

Ingredients:

» 1 cup of freshly brewed hot coffee
» 1 ounce of irish cream liqueur
» 1 ounce of hazelnut liqueur
» For topping whipped cream
» A pinch of ground cinnamon or nutmeg (for garnish)
» Chocolate shavings or hazelnuts (chopped, optional, for garnish)

Preparation Time:
7 minutes

Directions:

1. Brew Coffee: Begin by brewing your favorite coffee. A medium or dark roast works well for this recipe, as it provides a robust flavor that complements the liqueurs.
2. Prepare the Mug: Warm your coffee mug by rinsing it with hot water. This helps to keep your coffee hot for a longer period.
3. Combine Coffee and Liqueurs: Pour the freshly brewed hot coffee into the warmed mug. Add the Irish cream liqueur and hazelnut liqueur to the coffee and stir gently to combine.
4. Add Whipped Cream: Top the coffee with a generous amount of whipped cream. The cream will float on top, creating a deliciously creamy layer.
5. Garnish: Sprinkle a pinch of ground cinnamon or nutmeg over the whipped cream. For an extra touch of indulgence, add chocolate shavings or chopped hazelnuts as garnish.
6. Serve the Nutty Irishman Coffee immediately, offering a spoon to enjoy the creamy top layer along with the rich, liqueur-infused coffee.

3.4 Warm and Cozy Coffees for Chilly Evenings

16 MAPLE PECAN COFFEE

Maple Pecan Coffee is a delightful and aromatic drink that combines the rich, deep flavors of coffee with the warm sweetness of maple syrup and the nutty essence of pecans. This beverage is perfect for those who enjoy a hint of natural sweetness and nuttiness in their coffee

Ingredients:
- » 1 cup of freshly brewed hot coffee
- » 2 tablespoons of maple syrup
- » ½ teaspoon of pecan extract (or use finely ground pecans)
- » Whipped cream (optional, for topping)
- » Crushed pecans (optional, for garnish)
- » Cinnamon powder (optional, for garnish)

Preparation Time:
8 minutes

Directions:
1. Brew Coffee: Start by brewing your favorite coffee. A medium or dark roast is ideal, as it will complement the sweetness of the maple syrup and the flavor of the pecans.
2. Add Maple Syrup and Pecan Flavor: Once the coffee is brewed, stir in the maple syrup and pecan extract. If you're using ground pecans, ensure they are finely ground so they can blend well with the coffee. Adjust the amount of maple syrup to suit your taste preference.
3. Heat and Froth (Optional): If you prefer a frothy top, you can heat a small amount of milk or cream and froth it using a frother or by whisking vigorously.
4. Assemble the Drink: Pour the flavored coffee into a mug. If you've frothed some milk or cream, spoon it on top of the coffee.
5. Add Toppings: For added indulgence, top with whipped cream. Sprinkle crushed pecans and a dash of cinnamon powder over the whipped cream for extra flavor and a decorative touch.
6. Serve the Maple Pecan Coffee immediately, and enjoy the harmonious blend of sweet, nutty flavors with your rich, hot coffee.

17 HAZELNUT HOT COFFEE

Hazelnut Hot Coffee is a cozy and aromatic drink that combines the rich, bold flavors of coffee with the sweet, nutty essence of hazelnut. This beverage is perfect for coffee lovers who enjoy a hint of nutty sweetness in their cup.

Ingredients:

» 1 cup of freshly brewed hot coffee
» 2 tablespoons of hazelnut syrup (adjust to taste)
» ¼ cup milk or cream (optional, for creaminess)
» Whipped cream (optional, for topping)
» Crushed hazelnuts or chocolate shavings (optional, for garnish)

Preparation Time:
10 minutes

Directions:

1. Brew Coffee: Begin by brewing your favorite coffee. Choose a medium or dark roast to complement the hazelnut flavor.
2. Warm Milk or Cream: If you're adding milk or cream for extra creaminess, heat it gently in a saucepan or the microwave until warm. Avoid boiling to maintain a smooth texture.
3. Add Hazelnut Flavor: Stir the hazelnut syrup into the hot coffee. Adjust the amount of syrup based on how sweet or nutty you prefer your coffee.
4. Combine with Milk or Cream: If using, add the warm milk or cream to the hazelnut-flavored coffee and stir well to combine.
5. Top with Whipped Cream: For an added treat, top your coffee with a dollop of whipped cream.
6. Garnish: Sprinkle crushed hazelnuts or chocolate shavings over the whipped cream for a decorative and flavorful touch.
7. Serve the Hazelnut Hot Coffee immediately, offering a perfect blend of warmth, sweetness, and nuttiness in every sip.

18 BUTTERSCOTCH BREW

Butterscotch Brew is a rich and indulgent coffee drink that combines the deep flavors of coffee with the sweet, buttery taste of butterscotch. This delightful beverage is perfect for those who enjoy a creamy and sweet twist on their regular cup of coffee.

Ingredients:
» 1 cup of freshly brewed hot coffee
» 2 tablespoons of butterscotch syrup (adjust to taste)
» ¼ cup of milk or cream
» Whipped cream (optional, for topping)
» Butterscotch chips or drizzle (optional, for garnish)
» A pinch of sea salt (optional, for enhancing flavor)

Preparation Time:
10 minutes

Directions:
1. Brew Coffee: Start by brewing your preferred coffee. A medium or dark roast coffee is recommended to balance the sweetness of the butterscotch.
2. Heat Milk or Cream: In a small saucepan or the microwave, heat the milk or cream until warm. Be careful not to boil it to maintain a smooth texture.
3. Add Butterscotch Flavor: Pour the butterscotch syrup into the hot coffee and stir well to combine. Adjust the amount of syrup based on your preference for sweetness.
4. Combine with Milk or Cream: Add the warmed milk or cream to the butterscotch-flavored coffee and stir well.
5. Top with Whipped Cream: If desired, add a generous dollop of whipped cream to the top of your coffee.
6. Garnish: Sprinkle butterscotch chips or drizzle butterscotch syrup over the whipped cream. For a unique twist, add a pinch of sea salt to enhance the butterscotch flavor.
7. Serve your Butterscotch Brew immediately, savoring the creamy, buttery, and sweet flavors that make this drink a delightful treat.

3.5 Vegan Delights

19 CLASSIC VEGAN LATTE

The Classic Vegan Latte is a dairy-free alternative to the traditional latte, using plant-based milk to create a smooth, creamy, and flavorful coffee drink. It's perfect for vegans, lactose-intolerant individuals, or anyone looking to enjoy a delicious dairy-free coffee option.

Ingredients:
- » 1 shot of espresso or strong brewed coffee
- » 1 cup of plant-based milk (such as almond milk, soy milk, oat milk, or coconut milk)
- » To taste sweetener of choice (such as agave syrup, maple syrup, or sugar) (optional)
- » Cinnamon or cocoa powder (optional, for garnish)

Preparation Time:
8 minutes

Directions:
1. Brew Espresso/Coffee: Start by brewing a shot of espresso. If you don't have an espresso machine, you can use a strong brewed coffee as an alternative. A dark roast is preferable for a richer flavor.
2. Heat and Froth Plant-Based Milk: Heat the plant-based milk in a saucepan over medium heat until hot but not boiling. Froth the milk using a milk frother. If you don't have a frother, you can use a whisk or blend the milk in a blender to create foam. Oat milk and soy milk are excellent for frothing, while almond and coconut milk will give a lighter foam.
3. Combine Coffee and Milk: Pour the freshly brewed espresso or coffee into a large mug. Slowly add the frothed plant-based milk to the coffee. Hold back the foam with a spoon at first, then scoop it on top.
4. Sweeten (Optional): If desired, sweeten your latte with agave syrup, maple syrup, or sugar to taste.
5. Garnish: Sprinkle a bit of cinnamon or cocoa powder on top for an extra touch of flavor and a beautiful presentation.
6. Enjoy: Serve the Classic Vegan Latte immediately, stirring gently if you've added sweetener, and enjoy the rich, creamy texture and robust flavor.

20 TURMERIC LATTE WITH ESPRESSO

The Turmeric Latte with Espresso, often referred to as a "Golden Espresso Latte," is a healthful and invigorating drink that combines the earthy, spicy flavors of turmeric with the rich intensity of espresso. This beverage is perfect for those seeking a caffeine kick coupled with the potential health benefits of turmeric.

Ingredients:

» 1 shot of espresso or strong brewed coffee
» 1 cup milk (plant-based milk like almond, soy, or oat milk)
» Turmeric powder
» A pinch ground ginger
» ¼ teaspoon of ground cinnamon
» A pinch of black pepper (to enhance turmeric absorption)
» 1 tablespoon of honey or sweetener of choice (optional)
» ½ teaspoon of vanilla extract (optional)

Preparation Time:
10 minutes

Directions:

1. Brew Espresso/Coffee: Start by brewing a shot of espresso. If you don't have an espresso machine, strong-brewed coffee can be used as an alternative.
2. Prepare Turmeric Mixture: In a small saucepan, combine the milk, turmeric powder, ground ginger, ground cinnamon, and a pinch of black pepper. If using, add the honey and vanilla extract for added sweetness and flavor. The black pepper is used to enhance the absorption of curcumin, the active ingredient in turmeric.
3. Heat the Mixture: Heat the mixture over medium heat while stirring constantly. Do not bring it to a boil but let it become hot enough for the flavors to meld together.
4. Froth the Milk: Once the turmeric mixture is hot, use a milk frother to froth the milk to your desired level of foaminess. If you don't have a frother, whisk vigorously or use a blender, taking care with the hot liquid.
5. Combine with Espresso: Pour the brewed espresso into a large mug. Gently pour the frothed turmeric milk over the espresso.
6. Garnish: Sprinkle a little bit of ground cinnamon on top for a warming, aromatic finish.
7. Enjoy: Serve the Turmeric Latte with Espresso immediately, stirring gently before sipping to blend the flavors.

21 GINGERBREAD CASHEW COFFEE

The Gingerbread Cashew Coffee is a festive and flavorful beverage that combines the warm, spicy essence of gingerbread with the creamy, nutty notes of cashew. It's an ideal drink for the holiday season or anytime you crave a comforting and unique coffee experience.

Ingredients:

Preparation Time:
12 minutes

- » 1 cup of freshly brewed hot coffee
- » ½ cup of cashew milk
- » 1 tablespoon of molasses
- » ½ teaspoon of ground ginger
- » ½ teaspoon of ground cinnamon
- » A pinch of ground nutmeg
- » A pinch of ground cloves
- » ¼ teaspoon of vanilla extract
- » Whipped cream (optional, for topping)
- » Crushed cashews (optional, for garnish)
- » Additional cinnamon or gingerbread spice (optional, for garnish)

Directions:

1. Brew Coffee: Start by brewing your preferred coffee. A medium or dark roast is recommended to balance the spices' flavors.
2. Heat and Spice Cashew Milk: In a small saucepan, combine the cashew milk, molasses, ground ginger, cinnamon, nutmeg, cloves, and vanilla extract. Heat the mixture over medium heat, stirring constantly, until hot but not boiling. The aim is to infuse the milk with the gingerbread spices and molasses.
3. Froth Milk Mixture: Once the milk is hot and the spices are well incorporated, use a milk frother to create a frothy texture. If you don't have a frother, you can whisk it vigorously by hand or blend it for a few seconds in a blender, taking care of the hot liquid.
4. Combine with Coffee: Pour the freshly brewed hot coffee into a large mug. Gently add the spiced cashew milk mixture to the coffee.
5. Top with Whipped Cream: Optionally, add a dollop of whipped cream on top of your gingerbread cashew coffee.
6. Garnish: Sprinkle crushed cashews and additional cinnamon or gingerbread spice over the whipped cream for extra flavor and a festive look.
7. Enjoy: Serve the Gingerbread Cashew Coffee immediately, stirring gently to blend the flavors before sipping.

22 CARAMEL HEMP LATTE

The Caramel Hemp Latte is a delightful and nutritious twist on the classic latte, incorporating the nutty, earthy flavors of hemp milk with the sweet, buttery taste of caramel. This latte is an excellent choice for those seeking a dairy-free and vegan-friendly coffee option that doesn't compromise on taste.

Ingredients:
» 1 shot of espresso or strong brewed coffee
» 1 cup of hemp milk
» 2 tablespoons of caramel syrup (adjust to taste)
» ¼ teaspoon of vanilla extract (optional)
» Whipped coconut cream (optional, for topping)
» Additional caramel syrup or caramel drizzle (optional, for garnish)

Preparation Time:
11 minutes

Directions:
1. Brew Espresso/Coffee: Start by brewing a shot of espresso. If you don't have an espresso machine, you can make a strong brewed coffee as an alternative. A dark roast is ideal for a richer flavor.
2. Heat and Froth Hemp Milk: In a small saucepan, heat the hemp milk over medium heat until it's hot but not boiling. Froth the hemp milk using a milk frother. If you don't have a frother, you can use a whisk or blend the milk in a blender to create foam. Hemp milk froths differently than dairy milk, so it might not be as thick.
3. Flavor the Milk: Stir the caramel syrup and vanilla extract (if using) into the heated hemp milk. Mix well until the caramel is fully dissolved and the flavors are combined.
4. Combine with Coffee: Pour the freshly brewed espresso or coffee into a large mug. Slowly add the frothed caramel-flavored hemp milk to the coffee.
5. Top with Whipped Cream: Optionally, add a dollop of whipped coconut cream on top of your latte for added richness and flavor.
6. Garnish: Drizzle additional caramel syrup or caramel drizzle over the whipped cream for an extra touch of sweetness and a visually appealing finish.
7. Enjoy Serve your Caramel Hemp Latte immediately, stirring gently before sipping to blend the flavors.

23 LAVENDER ALMOND MACCHIATO

The Lavender Almond Macchiato is a delicate and aromatic coffee drink that combines the rich taste of espresso with the soothing floral notes of lavender and the nutty sweetness of almonds. This elegant beverage is perfect for those who enjoy a sophisticated twist on their coffee.

Ingredients:

» 1 shot of espresso or strong brewed coffee
» 1 cup of almond milk
» 1 tablespoon of lavender syrup (adjust to taste)
» Dried culinary lavender flowers (optional, for garnish)
» Almond slices or almond extract (optional, for enhanced flavor)
» Honey or sweetener of choice (optional, for added sweetness)

Preparation Time:
9 minutes

Directions:

1. Brew Espresso/Coffee: Begin by brewing a shot of espresso. If you don't have an espresso machine, strong-brewed coffee can be used as an alternative. A dark roast is preferable for a richer flavor.
2. Heat and Froth Almond Milk: In a small saucepan, heat the almond milk over medium heat until it's hot but not boiling. Froth the almond milk using a milk frother. If you don't have a frother, you can whisk it vigorously or blend it in a blender to create foam. Almond milk froths differently than dairy milk, so the foam might be less dense.
3. Flavor the Milk: Stir in the lavender syrup to the heated almond milk. If using almond extract, add a few drops for a nuttier flavor. Adjust the amount of syrup or extract based on your taste preference. You can also sweeten it with honey or your choice of sweetener.
4. Assemble the Macchiato: Pour the freshly brewed espresso or coffee into a large mug. Carefully spoon the frothed lavender almond milk over the coffee, creating a layered effect.
5. Garnish: Sprinkle a few dried lavender flowers on top for an aromatic and visually appealing finish. Optionally, add almond slices for extra texture and flavor.
6. Enjoy: Serve the Lavender Almond Macchiato immediately, offering a unique blend of floral, nutty, and coffee flavors in each sip.

24 SPICED PUMPKIN OAT LATTE

The Spiced Pumpkin Oat Latte is a cozy and flavorful beverage that encapsulates the essence of autumn. Combining the rich taste of coffee with the creamy texture of oat milk and the seasonal flavors of pumpkin and spices, this latte is perfect for those crisp fall days.

Ingredients:

» 2 shot of espresso or strong brewed coffee
» 1 cup of oat milk
» 2 tablespoons of pumpkin puree
» ½ teaspoon of pumpkin pie spice
» ¼ teaspoon of vanilla extract
» 1 tablespoon of maple syrup or sweetener of choice (adjust to taste)
» Whipped cream (optional, for topping)
» A pinch of cinnamon or extra pumpkin pie spice (optional, for garnish)

Preparation Time:
12 minutes

Directions:

1. Brew Espresso/Coffee: Start by brewing two shots of espresso. If you don't have an espresso machine, you can use strong brewed coffee instead.
2. Heat and Spice Oat Milk: In a small saucepan, combine the oat milk, pumpkin puree, pumpkin pie spice, and vanilla extract. Heat the mixture over medium heat, stirring constantly, until it is hot but not boiling. This process allows the flavors to meld together and the pumpkin to dissolve into the milk.
3. Sweeten the Mixture: Add maple syrup or your chosen sweetener to the pumpkin-oat milk mixture. Stir well to ensure it's fully incorporated.
4. Froth the Milk: Once the mixture is hot, use a milk frother to froth the milk to your desired level of foaminess. If you don't have a frother, you can whisk it vigorously by hand or blend it in a blender for a few seconds.
5. Combine with Coffee: Pour the freshly brewed espresso or coffee into a large mug. Gently pour the frothed spiced pumpkin oat milk over the coffee.
6. Top with Whipped Cream: Optionally, add a dollop of whipped cream on top of your latte for added richness.
7. Garnish: Sprinkle a pinch of cinnamon or extra pumpkin pie spice on top of the whipped cream for an aromatic and visually appealing finish.
8. Enjoy: Serve the Spiced Pumpkin Oat Latte immediately, stirring gently before sipping to blend the flavors together.

3.6 Health-Conscious Blends

25 PROTEIN-PACKED COFFEE SHAKE

The Protein-Packed Coffee Shake is a robust and nutritious drink that combines the energizing effects of coffee with the sustaining power of protein. This shake is perfect for a post-workout boost, a filling breakfast, or a midday pick-me-up that offers both nutrition and flavor.

Ingredients:

» 1 cup of cold brew coffee or chilled espresso
» 1 scoop of protein powder (whey or plant-based)
» Banana: 1, preferably frozen
» ½ cup of almond milk or milk of choice
» ½ cup of greek yogurt or plant-based yogurt (for additional protein and creaminess)
» 1 tablespoon of peanut butter or almond butter
» ½ cup of ice cubes
» 1 teaspoon of cocoa powder (optional, for chocolate flavor)
» To taste honey or maple syrup (optional, for sweetness)
» A pinch of cinnamon (optional, for extra flavor)

Preparation Time:
10 minutes

Directions:

1. Prepare Coffee: If you're using cold brew coffee, ensure it's chilled. If using espresso, brew it ahead of time and let it cool in the refrigerator.
2. Blend Ingredients: In a blender, combine the cold brew coffee or chilled espresso, protein powder, frozen banana, almond milk, Greek or plant-based yogurt, peanut or almond butter, ice cubes, and cocoa powder (if using).
3. Add Sweeteners/Flavorings: Add honey or maple syrup for sweetness if desired. Include a pinch of cinnamon for added flavor.
4. Blend Until Smooth: Blend all the ingredients on high speed until the shake is smooth and creamy. Ensure there are no lumps, and the consistency is even.
5. Adjust Thickness: If the shake is too thick, add a little more almond milk or coffee to thin it out. If it's too thin, add a few more ice cubes and blend again.
6. Serve: Pour the shake into a large glass and serve immediately.

26 KETO BULLETPROOF COFFEE

Keto Bulletproof Coffee, also known as butter coffee, is a popular drink in the ketogenic diet community. It's known for its ability to provide sustained energy and help with mental clarity. This coffee is made by blending traditional coffee with healthy fats, specifically grass-fed butter and medium-chain triglyceride (MCT) oil. It's a perfect breakfast drink for those on a keto diet or anyone looking for a filling, energizing coffee.

Ingredients:

» 1 cup of freshly brewed hot coffee
» 1 to 2 tablespoons of grass-fed unsalted butter
» 1 tablespoon MCT oil or coconut oil
» Optional: Heavy cream, cinnamon, or vanilla extract for added flavor

Preparation Time:
5 minutes

Directions:

1. Brew Coffee: Begin by brewing a cup of your favorite coffee. A stronger brew works well for this recipe as it balances the richness of the fats.
2. Gather Your Ingredients: Measure out the grass-fed butter and MCT oil. The butter should be unsalted, and the oil should be pure MCT or coconut oil for the best results.
3. Blend the Ingredients: Pour the hot coffee into a blender. Add the measured butter and MCT oil. If you're adding optional ingredients like heavy cream, cinnamon, or vanilla extract for flavor, include them at this stage.
4. Blend Until Creamy: Blend the mixture on high for about 30 seconds or until it becomes a creamy, homogeneous concoction. The coffee should look frothy and light, similar to a latte.
5. Serve Immediately: Pour the blended coffee into a mug and serve it immediately. It's best enjoyed hot.

27 AVOCADO COFFEE SMOOTHIE

The Avocado Coffee Smoothie is a creamy, nutritious, and energizing beverage, perfect for those looking for a filling and healthy coffee option. This smoothie combines the rich taste of coffee with the creamy texture of avocado, along with added sweetness and flavor, making it an ideal breakfast or snack.

Ingredients:
- » 1 cup of strongly brewed coffee, cooled
- » ½ pitted and scooped ripe avocado
- » 1 preferably frozen banana
- » ½ cup of almond milk or milk of choice
- » 1 tablespoon of honey or maple syrup (adjust to taste)
- » ½ teaspoon of vanilla extract
- » ½ cup of ice cubes
- » 1 teaspoon of cocoa powder (optional, for a chocolate flavor)
- » A pinch of ground cinnamon (optional, for extra flavor)

Preparation Time:
10 minutes

Directions:
1. Prepare Coffee: Brew a cup of strong coffee and allow it to cool. You can do this ahead of time and store the coffee in the refrigerator.
2. Combine Ingredients in Blender: In a blender, add the cooled coffee, ripe avocado, frozen banana, almond milk, honey (or maple syrup), vanilla extract, and ice cubes. If you're using cocoa powder and cinnamon, add them as well.
3. Blend Until Smooth: Blend all the ingredients on high speed until the mixture is smooth and creamy. Make sure there are no lumps and the consistency is even.
4. Adjust Thickness and Taste: If the smoothie is too thick, add a little more almond milk or coffee to thin it out. If it's not sweet enough for your taste, add a bit more honey or maple syrup.
5. Serve Immediately: Pour the smoothie into a glass and serve immediately.

28 MACA MOCHA

The Maca Mocha is a unique and energizing beverage that blends the rich flavors of a classic mocha with the health benefits of maca powder. Maca, a root native to Peru, is known for its nutrient-rich profile and natural energy-boosting properties. This drink is perfect for coffee lovers looking for an extra health kick in their daily brew.

Ingredients:

» 1 shot of freshly brewed espresso or strong coffee
» 1 cup of milk (dairy or plant-based)
» 1 tablespoon of cocoa powder
» 1 teaspoon of maca powder
» To taste maple syrup or sweetener of choice
» Dark chocolate shavings or cocoa powder (optional, for garnish)
» Whipped cream (optional, for topping)

Preparation Time:
11 minutes

Directions:

1. Brew Espresso/Coffee: Start by brewing a shot of espresso or a small cup of strong coffee. A rich, dark roast is ideal for the mocha flavor profile.
2. Heat and Froth Milk: In a saucepan, heat the milk over medium heat until it's hot but not boiling. Froth the milk using a milk frother for a creamy texture. If you don't have a frother, you can whisk it vigorously by hand or blend it in a blender for a few seconds.
3. Mix Cocoa and Maca Powder: In a small bowl, mix the cocoa powder and maca powder. Add a little hot water or milk to form a smooth paste. This step helps prevent clumps of cocoa or maca in your drink.
4. Combine Ingredients: Pour the cocoa-maca mixture into a large mug. Add the freshly brewed espresso or coffee and stir well. Sweeten with maple syrup or your preferred sweetener to taste.
5. Add Frothed Milk: Gently pour the frothed milk into the mug, stirring gently to blend everything together.
6. Garnish and Serve: Optionally, top with whipped cream and sprinkle with dark chocolate shavings or a dusting of cocoa powder. Serve your Maca Mocha hot and enjoy the rich, chocolaty flavor with a boost of natural energy from the maca powder.

29 COCOA CITRUS COFFEE ZEST

Cocoa Citrus Coffee Zest is an invigorating and flavorful beverage that combines the rich depth of coffee with the bright, refreshing notes of citrus and the warm comfort of cocoa. This unique drink is perfect for those looking to add a twist to their coffee routine.

Ingredients:

Preparation Time:
10 minutes

- » 1 cup of freshly brewed hot coffee
- » 1 tablespoon of unsweetened cocoa powder
- » 1 teaspoon of orange zest finely grated
- » 1 teaspoon of lemon zest finely grated
- » 1 tablespoon of brown sugar or sweetener of choice (adjust to taste)
- » ¼ cup of milk or cream (optional, for creaminess)
- » Whipped cream (optional, for topping)
- » Additional orange or lemon zest (optional, for garnish)
- » A pinch of cinnamon or nutmeg (optional, for extra spice)

Directions:
1. Brew Coffee: Begin by brewing a cup of your favorite coffee. A medium or dark roast works well for this recipe, as it complements the cocoa and citrus flavors.
2. Prepare Citrus Zest: Wash an orange and a lemon thoroughly. Using a fine grater or zester, grate about one teaspoon each of orange and lemon zest. Be careful to avoid the white pith, as it can be bitter.
3. Mix Cocoa and Zest with Coffee: In your coffee cup, combine the hot coffee, cocoa powder, orange zest, lemon zest, and brown sugar or sweetener. Stir well until the cocoa powder is completely dissolved and the ingredients are well blended.
4. Heat and Froth Milk (Optional): If you prefer a creamier coffee, heat the milk or cream in a small saucepan or microwave until warm. Froth it using a milk frother or by whisking vigorously.
5. Combine with Coffee: If using milk or cream, pour it into the coffee mixture and stir well.
6. Garnish and Serve: Top with whipped cream if desired. Garnish with additional orange or lemon zest and a pinch of cinnamon or nutmeg for a warm, spicy finish.
7. Enjoy: Serve the Cocoa Citrus Coffee Zest immediately, savoring the unique combination of rich coffee, tangy citrus, and comforting cocoa.

30 NUTTY HEMP COFFEE

Nutty Hemp Coffee is a delightful and healthful twist on traditional coffee. This recipe infuses the rich, deep flavors of coffee with the nutty essence of hemp seeds and hemp milk. It's a fantastic choice for those seeking a dairy-free coffee option with an added nutritional boost.

Ingredients:

- » 1 cup of freshly brewed hot coffee
- » ½ cup of hemp milk
- » 2 tablespoons of hemp seeds (shelled, also known as hemp hearts)
- » 1 tablespoon of almond butter or nut butter of choice
- » To taste maple syrup or sweetener of choice
- » ½ teaspoon of vanilla extract (optional)
- » A pinch of cinnamon (optional, for garnish)
- » Whipped coconut cream (optional, for topping)

Preparation Time:
12 minutes

Directions:

1. Brew Coffee: Begin by brewing your favorite coffee. A medium or dark roast is ideal for this recipe, as it complements the nutty flavors.
2. Prepare Hemp Milk Mixture: In a small saucepan, gently heat the hemp milk. You want it to be warm but not boiling. If you prefer a frothier texture, you can froth the hemp milk using a milk frother or a blender.
3. Blend Coffee with Hemp Seeds and Almond Butter: In a blender, combine the hot coffee, hemp seeds, almond butter, and, if using, vanilla extract. Hemp seeds add a mild, nutty flavor and a boost of nutrition.
4. Sweeten the Coffee: Add maple syrup or your preferred sweetener to the blender. The amount can be adjusted according to your taste preferences.
5. Blend Until Smooth: Blend the mixture on high speed until it's smooth and creamy. Ensure that the hemp seeds and almond butter are well integrated, creating a uniform texture.
6. Serve: Pour the blended coffee into a mug. If you used a milk frother, add the frothed hemp milk on top.
7. Garnish: Optionally, top with whipped coconut cream. Sprinkle a pinch of cinnamon over the top for a warm, aromatic finish.
8. Enjoy: Your Nutty Hemp Coffee is now ready to be enjoyed. It offers a wonderful combination of rich coffee flavor with the creamy, nutty nuances of hemp and almond.

3.7 Low-Caffeine Options for Sensitive Coffee Lovers

31 HALF-CAF HONEY VANILLA LATTE

The Half-Caf Honey Vanilla Latte is a delightful coffee drink that offers the perfect balance of caffeine and flavor. It's made with half-caffeinated coffee, which is ideal for those who enjoy the taste of coffee but are sensitive to caffeine. The addition of honey and vanilla gives it a natural sweetness and a warm, comforting aroma.

Ingredients:
» 1 shot of espresso of half-caffeinated coffee beans or ground coffee
» 1 cup of milk (dairy or any plant-based alternative)
» 2 tablespoons of honey (adjust to taste)
» ½ teaspoon of vanilla extract
» Whipped cream (optional, for topping)
» Cinnamon or cocoa powder (optional, for garnish)

Preparation Time:
7 minutes

Directions:
1. Brew Half-Caf Espresso/Coffee: Start by brewing a shot of espresso using half-caffeinated coffee. If you don't have an espresso machine, you can use a strong half-caffeinated coffee made in a regular coffee maker. Half-caffeinated coffee is typically a blend of 50% caffeinated and 50% decaffeinated beans.
2. Heat and Froth Milk: In a saucepan, heat the milk over medium heat until it's hot but not boiling. Froth the milk using a milk frother for a creamy texture. If you don't have a frother, you can whisk it vigorously by hand or blend it in a blender.
3. Sweeten with Honey and Vanilla: In a separate small bowl or cup, mix the honey and vanilla extract. Add a little bit of the hot milk to dissolve the honey and mix well.
4. Combine Coffee, Milk, and Honey-Vanilla Mixture: Pour the honey-vanilla mixture into a large mug. Add the brewed espresso or coffee and stir well. Gently pour the frothed milk into the mug, stirring gently to blend.
5. Garnish and Serve: Optionally, top with whipped cream and sprinkle with cinnamon or cocoa powder for an extra touch of flavor and elegance.
6. Enjoy: Your Half-Caf Honey Vanilla Latte is ready to enjoy. It offers a gentler caffeine kick, combined with the soothing flavors of honey and vanilla.

32 GENTLE MOCHA SWIRL

The Gentle Mocha Swirl is a smooth and inviting coffee beverage that combines the rich flavors of chocolate and coffee with a delicate touch. It's a milder version of the classic mocha, perfect for those who enjoy a less intense coffee experience with all the comforting chocolatey goodness.

Ingredients:

- » 1 cup of freshly brewed coffee
- » ½ cup of milk (dairy or plant-based)
- » 1 tablespoon of cocoa powder
- » 1 tablespoon of sugar or sweetener of choice (adjust to taste)
- » Whipped cream (optional, for topping)
- » Chocolate syrup or melted chocolate (optional, for drizzling)
- » ½ teaspoon of vanilla extract

Preparation Time:
10 minutes

Directions:

1. Brew Coffee: Start by brewing your coffee. Choose a light to medium roast for a gentler flavor profile.
2. Heat Milk: In a saucepan, gently heat the milk over medium heat. Avoid boiling. If you prefer a frothy mocha, you can froth the milk using a milk frother or by whisking vigorously.
3. Mix Cocoa and Sugar: In a small bowl, mix the cocoa powder and sugar (or your choice of sweetener). Add a little bit of the hot milk to form a smooth paste. This helps to avoid clumps of cocoa in your drink.
4. Combine Coffee and Cocoa Mixture: Pour the cocoa-sugar mixture into your coffee and stir well until fully dissolved. Add vanilla extract for an extra layer of flavor.
5. Add Milk: Gently pour the heated (and optionally frothed) milk into the coffee and cocoa mixture. Stir to combine everything evenly.
6. Top with Whipped Cream: If desired, top your Gentle Mocha Swirl with a dollop of whipped cream for a luxurious touch.
7. Drizzle with Chocolate: For a decadent finish, drizzle chocolate syrup or melted chocolate over the whipped cream.
8. Enjoy: Serve the Gentle Mocha Swirl immediately, offering a harmonious blend of coffee, chocolate, and creamy milk.

33 DECAF CITRUS ZEST AMERICANO

The Decaf Citrus Zest Americano is a refreshing and aromatic twist on the classic Americano. By incorporating citrus zest, this decaffeinated version offers a vibrant and flavorful experience without the caffeine. It's perfect for evenings or for those who are sensitive to caffeine but still enjoy the taste of coffee.

Ingredients:

» 2 shots of decaffeinated espresso or strong decaf coffee
» 1 cup of hot water
» 1 teaspoon of orange zest finely grated
» 1 teaspoon of lemon zest finely grated
» To taste sugar or sweetener of choice (optional)
» Ice cubes (for iced version, optional)
» Lemon or orange slice (for garnish, optional)

Preparation Time:
12 minutes

Directions:

1. Brew Decaf Espresso/Coffee: Begin by brewing two shots of decaffeinated espresso. If you don't have an espresso machine, use a strong brewed decaffeinated coffee.
2. Prepare Citrus Zest: Wash an orange and a lemon thoroughly. Using a fine grater or zester, grate about one teaspoon each of orange and lemon zest. Be careful to avoid the white pith, as it can be bitter.
3. Hot Version:
   - Combine Espresso and Hot Water: In a large coffee cup, combine the hot decaf espresso or coffee with hot water to create an Americano base.
   - Add Citrus Zest: Stir in the orange and lemon zest. Mix well to infuse the citrus flavors into the drink.
   - Sweeten (Optional): Add sugar or your preferred sweetener, if desired, and stir well.
   - Enjoy: Serve hot, garnished with a slice of lemon or orange, if desired.
4. Iced Version:
   - Chill the Espresso/Coffee If you prefer an iced version, chill the brewed espresso or coffee in the refrigerator.
   - Prepare in a Glass: Fill a tall glass with ice cubes. Pour the chilled decaf espresso or coffee over the ice.
   - Add Citrus Zest and Cold Water: Stir in the orange and lemon zest, and then add cold water. Stir well.
   - Sweeten and Garnish (Optional): Sweeten as desired and garnish with a lemon or orange slice.

34 LOW-CAF ALMOND MILK MISTO

The Low-Caf Almond Milk Misto is a comforting and health-conscious coffee drink, ideal for those who prefer a lower caffeine intake but still enjoy the warmth and flavor of coffee. This beverage blends the mild taste of low-caffeine coffee with the creamy texture of almond milk, creating a soothing and enjoyable experience.

Ingredients:

- » Enough for 1 cup of brewed coffee low-caffeine coffee grounds
- » 1 cup of almond milk
- » ½ teaspoon of vanilla extract (optional)
- » To taste honey or sweetener of choice (optional)
- » Cinnamon or cocoa powder - for garnish (optional)

Preparation Time:
10 minutes

Directions:

1. Brew Low-Caf Coffee: Start by brewing your coffee using low-caffeine coffee grounds. You can use a drip coffee maker, French press, or any preferred brewing method. Low-caffeine coffee is typically a blend of regular and decaffeinated beans, offering about half the caffeine content of regular coffee.
2. Heat and Froth Almond Milk: Pour the almond milk into a saucepan and heat it over medium heat. Watch closely to ensure it doesn't boil. For a frothy Misto, use a milk frother to froth the almond milk to your desired level of foaminess. If you don't have a frother, you can whisk the milk vigorously or blend it briefly in a blender.
3. Add Flavor: If you're using vanilla extract or sweetener, add it to the almond milk and stir well.
4. Assemble the Misto: Fill a large mug halfway with the brewed low-caffeine coffee. Gently pour the heated (and optionally frothed) almond milk over the coffee. The ideal ratio is about 1:1, but you can adjust according to your preference.
5. Garnish and Serve: Sprinkle cinnamon or cocoa powder on top for an added touch of flavor and a beautiful presentation.
6. Enjoy: Your Low-Caf Almond Milk Misto is now ready to be enjoyed. It's perfect for those seeking a gentle caffeine boost and a dairy-free coffee experience.

ADVANCED QUICK COFFEE ARTS

4.1 Barista Secrets: Recipes to Impress Your Guests

35 VELVET ESPRESSO MARTINI

An elegant and sophisticated cocktail that combines the rich flavor of espresso with the smoothness of vodka and a hint of sweetness. It's a perfect choice for coffee lovers looking for an indulgent and luxurious cocktail experience.

Ingredients:

» 1 shot of freshly brewed espresso cooled
» 2 ounce of vodka
» 1 ounce of coffee liqueur (such as Kahlúa)
» ½ ounce of simple syrup (adjust to taste)
» Ice cubes
» Coffee beans (optional, for garnish)

Preparation Time:
10 minutes

Directions:

1. Brew and Cool Espresso: Start by brewing a shot of espresso. Allow it to cool to room temperature. You can brew the espresso ahead of time and refrigerate it to speed up the process.
2. Prepare Cocktail Shaker: Fill a cocktail shaker with ice cubes to chill the ingredients and create a frothy texture in the drink.
3. Combine Ingredients in Shaker: Add the cooled espresso, vodka, coffee liqueur, and simple syrup to the shaker. The simple syrup can be adjusted according to how sweet you like your cocktail.
4. Shake Vigorously: Seal the shaker and shake vigorously for about 10-15 seconds. Shaking not only chills the drink but also creates a nice frothy top.
5. Strain and Serve: Strain the cocktail into a chilled martini glass. The drink should have a creamy foam on top from the shaken espresso.
6. Garnish: For a classic and sophisticated presentation, garnish the martini with a few coffee beans floating on the foam.
7. Enjoy: Serve the Velvet Espresso Martini immediately. It's a delightful cocktail for an evening gathering, dinner party, or whenever you desire a coffee-infused elegant drink.

36 CASCARA FIZZ

An innovative and refreshing beverage that utilizes cascara, also known as coffee cherry tea, which is made from the dried skins of coffee cherries. This drink is a delightful combination of cascara's subtle fruity sweetness and sparkling water's enthusiasm, creating a unique and refreshing non-alcoholic beverage.

Ingredients:

» 2 tablespoons of dried cascara (coffee cherry tea)
» 1 cup of boiling water
» 1 cup of sparkling water
» 1 tablespoon of Honey or agave syrup (adjust to taste)
» 1 tablespoon of fresh lemon juice
» Ice cubes
» Lemon slice or mint leaves (for garnish)

Preparation Time:
15 minutes plus cooling time

Directions:

1. Steep the Cascara: Start by steeping the dried cascara in boiling water. Add the cascara to a heatproof container and pour the boiling water over it. Let it steep for about 10 minutes. This will extract the flavors and create a cascara tea base.
2. Strain and Cool: After steeping, strain the cascara tea into a pitcher or container to remove the solids. Let the tea cool to room temperature. For a quicker cooling process, you can place it in the refrigerator.
3. Sweeten the Tea: Once the cascara tea is cooled, stir in the honey or agave syrup until it's completely dissolved. Adjust the sweetness according to your preference.
4. Add Lemon Juice: Mix in the fresh lemon juice to add a bright, citrusy note to the drink.
5. Prepare the Drink: Fill a glass with ice cubes. Pour the cascara tea mixture over the ice, filling the glass about halfway.
6. Top with Sparkling Water: Slowly add sparkling water to fill the glass. This will create a fizzy effect, hence the name "Cascara Fizz."
7. Garnish and Serve: Garnish with a slice of lemon or a sprig of mint. Give the drink a gentle stir before serving.

37 SIPHON VANILLA SPICE COFFEE

A delightful and aromatic beverage that combines the unique brewing method of a siphon (or vacuum pot) with the warm flavors of vanilla and spices. This method of brewing creates a clean and crisp cup of coffee, while the vanilla and spices add a comforting and flavorful twist.

Ingredients:

Preparation Time:
12 minutes

» 2 tablespoons of ground coffee (medium to fine grind)
» 1 cup of water
» 1 Vanilla bean split lengthwise and seeds scraped
» ½ teaspoon of ground cinnamon
» A pinch of ground nutmeg
» 1 teaspoon of brown sugar or sweetener of choice (optional)

Directions:

1. Prepare the Siphon: Fill the bottom chamber of your siphon coffee maker with water. If your siphon has a cloth filter, attach it to the bottom of the upper chamber according to the manufacturer's instructions.
2. Add Vanilla and Spices to Water: Place the split vanilla bean (both pod and scraped seeds) into the water in the bottom chamber. Add the ground cinnamon and a pinch of nutmeg to the water as well.
3. Heat the Water: Position the siphon over its heat source, which could be a siphon burner, butane burner, or even a stovetop, depending on your siphon type. Heat the water until it's close to boiling, and you see it start to rise into the upper chamber.
4. Add Coffee Grounds: Once the water has risen into the upper chamber, add the ground coffee. Stir gently to ensure all the coffee grounds are fully immersed in the water.
5. Brew the Coffee: Allow the coffee to brew in the upper chamber for about 1 to 2 minutes. The exact time can vary based on your preference for strength.
6. Remove from Heat: After brewing, remove the siphon from the heat. As it cools, the brewed coffee will be drawn back down into the lower chamber, through the filter, leaving the grounds behind.
7. Sweeten (Optional): Once the brewed coffee is in the lower chamber, you can stir in brown sugar or your preferred sweetener if desired.
8. Serve: Pour the Vanilla Spice Coffee into cups, ensuring to leave the vanilla pod behind, and serve immediately.

38 COLD BREW OLD FASHIONED

A sophisticated and modern twist on the classic Old Fashioned cocktail, incorporating the rich depth of cold brew coffee. This cocktail is perfect for coffee enthusiasts and those who appreciate a well-crafted drink with a unique flavor profile.

Ingredients:
» 2 ounces of cold brew coffee concentrate
» 1.5 ounces of bourbon
» ½ ounce of simple syrup
» 2 dashes of angostura bitters
» Orange peel for garnish
» Ice cubes

Preparation Time:
5 minutes

Directions:
1. Prepare Cold Brew Concentrate: If you don't have ready-made cold brew concentrate, prepare it in advance by steeping coarsely ground coffee in cold water for 12-24 hours, then strain. For this recipe, a stronger concentrate works best.
2. Chill a Glass: Place an Old Fashioned glass in the freezer to chill it. A cold glass will enhance the drinking experience.
3. Combine Ingredients: In the chilled glass, add the cold brew coffee concentrate, bourbon, simple syrup, and two dashes of Angostura bitters.
4. Stir: Add a few ice cubes to the glass and stir the mixture gently for about 30 seconds. This not only chills the drink but also dilutes it slightly, mellowing the flavors.
5. Garnish: Express the oil of an orange peel over the drink by gently twisting it, then rim the glass with the peel to impart the aroma. Drop the peel into the glass as a garnish.
6. Immediately serve the cocktail: For the best experience, savor it slowly, allowing the flavors to develop with each sip.

39 NITRO COCONUT COFFEE

An exhilarating and creamy beverage that combines the smooth texture of nitro cold brew with the tropical sweetness of coconut. This drink is perfect for those seeking a refreshing and dairy-free alternative to traditional creamy coffee drinks.

Ingredients:

» 2 cups of cold brew coffee concentrate
» 1 cup of coconut water
» Nitrogen cartridge (for nitro coffee dispenser)
» Ice cubes (optional)

Preparation Time:
11 minutes (excluding time for making cold brew concentrate)

Directions:

1. Prepare Cold Brew Concentrate: If you don't have a ready-made cold brew concentrate, you'll need to prepare it in advance. Coarsely grind coffee beans and steep them in cold water for about 12-24 hours. After steeping, strain the coffee to get a clear concentration. This process can be done a day ahead.
2. Mix with Coconut Water: In a large pitcher or container, mix the cold brew coffee concentrate with coconut water. The coconut water adds a natural sweetness and a hint of tropical flavor to the coffee.
3. Chill the Mixture: Refrigerate the coffee and coconut water mixture until it is thoroughly chilled. This step is crucial for achieving the best texture and taste.
4. Prepare Nitro Coffee Dispenser: Fill your nitro coffee dispenser with the chilled coffee-coconut mixture. Make sure to follow the manufacturer's instructions for your specific nitro dispenser.
5. Charge with Nitrogen: Insert a nitrogen cartridge into the dispenser. Shake the dispenser vigorously for a few seconds to infuse the coffee with nitrogen. This process creates a rich, creamy head, similar to that of a stout beer.
6. Dispense into Glass: If you prefer your coffee cold, add a few ice cubes to a glass. Hold the nitro dispenser above the glass and dispense the coffee. You will see the beautiful cascading effect as the coffee fills the glass, topped with a creamy layer of foam.
7. Serve the Nitro Coconut Coffee immediately after dispensing. Enjoy the smooth, creamy texture with the subtle sweetness and refreshing flavor of coconut.

40 BOURBON BARREL AGED COFFEE

A unique and luxurious way to enjoy coffee, where the beans are aged in a used bourbon barrel. This process infuses the coffee beans with the rich, deep flavors of bourbon, oak, and vanilla without the alcohol content. The result is a complex, aromatic cup of coffee that's perfect for a special occasion or a sophisticated palate.

Ingredients:

» Bourbon barrel
» aged coffee beans
» Water – (Optional)
» Sweeteners or cream, as preferred

Preparation Time:
Varies based on the brewing method

Directions:

1. Select Your Brewing Method: Choose your preferred method of brewing. Bourbon barrel-aged coffee can be brewed using a French press, drip coffee maker, pour-over, or any other method you enjoy. Each method will extract different nuances from the beans.
2. Measure and Grind the Beans: Measure out the desired amount of bourbon barrel-aged coffee beans. A general guideline is about 1 to 2 tablespoons of coffee per 6 ounces of water, but you can adjust this ratio based on how strong you like your coffee. Grind the beans to the appropriate for your brewing method. For most methods, a medium grind is suitable.
3. Heat the Water: Heat your water to the correct temperature, which is generally around 195°F to 205°F (90°C to 96°C). Avoid boiling water, as it can scald the coffee and affect the flavor.
4. Brew the Coffee: Add the ground coffee to your coffee maker and pour the hot water over it. The brewing time will depend on your chosen method. For example, if using a French press, let the coffee steep for about 4 minutes before pressing.
5. Serve: Pour the freshly brewed bourbon barrel-aged coffee into a cup. Observe the unique aroma and note any distinct flavors imparted by the bourbon barrel aging process, such as hints of oak, vanilla, or caramel.
6. Enjoy the coffee black to appreciate the full range of flavors, or add cream or sweeteners to your liking.

41 PISTACHIO ROSE ESPRESSO

An exquisite and aromatic coffee drink that blends the rich intensity of espresso with the delicate flavors of pistachio and rose. This luxurious beverage is perfect for those who appreciate a floral and nutty twist to their espresso.

Ingredients:

Preparation Time:
5 minutes

»   1 shot of espresso
»   1 tablespoon of pistachio syrup
»   ½ teaspoon of rose water
»   ½ cup of milk (optional, for making a latte)
»   For garnish: Crushed pistachios
»   For garnish: dried rose petals (edible) Whipped cream (optional)

Directions:

1. Brew the Espresso: Start by brewing a shot of espresso using an espresso machine. If you don't have an espresso machine, you can make a strong coffee using a Moka pot or a similar brewing method.
2. Prepare Pistachio and Rose Mixture: In a cup, mix the pistachio syrup and rose water. Stir well to combine. These ingredients will provide a unique nutty and floral flavor to your espresso.
3. Combine Espresso with Flavored Mixture: Pour the freshly brewed espresso over the pistachio and rose mixture. Stir gently to infuse the flavors into the espresso.
4. Steam and Froth Milk (Optional for Latte): If you're making a latte, heat and froth the milk using a milk frother or by heating it on the stove and whisking until frothy. Pour the steamed, frothy milk over the flavored espresso.
5. Garnish your Pistachio Rose Espresso or Latte with crushed pistachios and a few dried rose petals. If desired, add a dollop of whipped cream on top for an extra luxurious touch.
6. Serve the beverage immediately, and enjoy the rich espresso combined with the distinct flavors of pistachio and rose.

4.2 Quick Latte Art Techniques for Stunning Presentations

42 THE HEART

Creating a heart in your latte is a classic and relatively simple way to begin practicing latte art. This technique adds an artistic touch to your coffee, making it more appealing and showing off your barista skills.

Ingredients:
- » 1 shot of freshly brewed espresso
- » 1 cup of steamed milk approximately
- » A pitcher for steaming milk
- » A latte cup (wide and shallow preferably)

Preparation Time:
5 minutes

Directions:
1. Prepare Espresso: Begin by brewing a shot of espresso into your latte cup. A good quality espresso with a nice crema on top is essential, as it serves as the canvas for your latte art.
2. Steam the Milk: Pour cold milk into a steaming pitcher. Use whole milk for the best results as its fat content creates smoother, more stable foam. Steam the milk with a steam wand until it reaches a silky, velvety texture, ideally between 140°F to 150°F (60°C to 65°C). Avoid creating too much foam; you're aiming for microfoam that is integrated with the milk.
3. Start Pouring the Milk: Hold the pitcher about three to four inches above the cup and start pouring the steamed milk into the center of the espresso. Pour steadily and smoothly. The milk should dive under the crema, creating a brown base on your cup.
4. Create the Heart Shape: Once your cup is about half full, bring the pitcher closer to the surface (about an inch above the cup). This is where you start creating the heart. Pour the milk faster and start wiggling the pitcher slightly back and forth. This motion will create a rounded, bulbous shape - the top of your heart.
5. Finish the Heart: As the cup fills, stop wiggling and raise the pitcher slightly, continuing to pour in a thin stream. This will draw a line through the middle of the rounded shape, forming the point of the heart.
6. Once your heart shape is complete, serve the latte immediately. The art looks best and is most distinct right after pouring.

43 THE ROSETTA

One of the most iconic and admired patterns in the world of latte art. It resembles a fern or a leaf and is created through a combination of pouring and delicate hand movement. Mastering the Rosetta can take some practice, but even beginners can achieve stunning results with a bit of patience and technique.

Ingredients:

» 1 shot of freshly brewed espresso
» Approximately 1 cup of steamed milk
» A pitcher for steaming milk
» A latte cup (wide and shallow preferably)

Preparation Time:
5 minutes

Directions:
1. Brew Espresso: Start by brewing a shot of espresso into your latte cup. A good crema on the espresso is essential as it will hold the design.
2. Steam the Milk: Fill a steaming pitcher with cold milk. Whole milk is generally preferred for its fat content which helps in creating smooth, velvety microfoam. Steam the milk to around 140°F to 150°F (60°C to 65°C), aiming for a silky texture without creating too much froth.
3. Begin Pouring the Milk: Hold the pitcher a few inches above the cup and start pouring the steamed milk into the center of the espresso. Pour steadily to mix the milk with the espresso and create a solid brown base in the cup.
4. Lower the Pitcher to Start the Rosetta: Once your cup is about half full, lower the pitcher close to the surface of the coffee, still pouring in the center. The closer you get, the more defined your pattern will be.
5. Create the Rosetta Pattern: Start moving the pitcher back and forth across the cup as you pour. This motion creates the leaves of the Rosetta. The key is to make small, quick side-to-side movements while steadily moving the pitcher backward towards you.
6. Finish the Rosetta: After you reach the far end of the cup, lift the pitcher slightly and pour a thin stream of milk through the center of the pattern you've created, all the way to the near end of the cup. This completes the Rosetta with a stem and gives it a more leaf-like appearance.
7. Present the freshly poured Rosetta latte art immediately for the best visual impact.

44 THE TULIP

A charming and popular latte art design characterized by its layered petal-like appearance. It's an impressive pattern that baristas often use to showcase their skill. With practice, you can create this beautiful design at home for an impressive presentation.

Ingredients:

» 1 shot of freshly brewed espresso
» 1 cup of steamed milk with silky microfoam
» A latte cup (wide and shallow is preferable)
» A milk steaming pitcher

Preparation Time:
5 minutes

Directions:

1. Brew Espresso: Begin by brewing a single shot of espresso directly into your latte cup. A good crema on top of the espresso is crucial as it will hold the latte art design.
2. Steam the Milk: Pour cold milk into a steaming pitcher. Whole milk is ideal for latte art due to its fat content, which helps in creating smooth and velvety microfoam. Steam the milk to a silky consistency, ideally between 140°F to 150°F (60°C to 65°C), ensuring you have enough microfoam.
3. Initial Pour: Start pouring the steamed milk into the center of the espresso from a height. This initial pour mixes the milk with the espresso. Gradually bring the pitcher closer to the surface as the cup fills up.
4. Begin the Tulip Design: Once the cup is about half full, lower the pitcher close to the surface of the coffee. Begin pouring slower and in place, which will create a small, white circle of foam – the first "petal" of the tulip.
5. Creating Petals: Lift the pitcher slightly and move it back slightly before pouring another petal. The second pour should push the first petal forward, creating the layered effect. Repeat this process, each time slightly retracting and then pouring another petal, pushing the previous ones forward.
6. Complete the Tulip: Once you have reached the desired number of layers (usually 3-5 petals), finish the design by dragging a thin line of milk through the center of the petals, from the back of the cup to the front. This creates the tulip's stem and gives the design a finished look.
7. Present the tulip latte art right away, showcasing the beautiful layered pattern.

45 THE SWAN

The Swan is an advanced and visually striking latte art design that resembles a graceful swan gliding on water. It's an elaborate variation of the more common Rosetta or Tulip designs and is sure to impress anyone who sees it. While it may seem complex, with a bit of practice, you can create this stunning piece of art in your coffee.

Ingredients:

» 1 shot of freshly brewed espresso
» 1 cup of steamed milk with silky microfoam
» A latte cup (wide and shallow is preferable)
» A milk steaming pitcher

Preparation Time:
5 minutes

Directions:

1. Prepare the Espresso: Brew a shot of espresso directly into your latte cup. Ensure that the espresso has a good crema, as this serves as the canvas for your latte art.
2. Steam the Milk: Pour cold milk into a steaming pitcher. Whole milk is recommended for its richness and ability to create a smooth microfoam. Steam the milk to achieve a glossy texture without creating large bubbles, ideally between 140°F to 150°F (60°C to 65°C).
3. Begin with the Base: Start pouring the steamed milk from a height into the center of the espresso, integrating the milk with the coffee. As the cup fills halfway, lower the pitcher close to the surface of the coffee and start pouring more slowly.
4. Create the Swan's Body: Pour a large bulb of milk (similar to creating the base of a heart) in the center of the cup. This will be the swan's body.
5. Form the Wings: Quickly sweep the pitcher back and forth while moving backward, creating the layered wing pattern on either side of the bulb. This motion is similar to creating a Rosetta.
6. Draw the Neck and Head: After completing the wings, lift the pitcher a little and create a thin line of milk from the bulb towards the edge of the cup, forming the swan's neck. As you reach the cup's rim, make a small loop back into the line to form the head.
7. Finish and Serve: Once the swan shape is complete, serve the coffee immediately to showcase your latte art skills.

46 THE WAVE HEART

The Wave Heart is a charming and visually appealing latte art design that combines the simplicity of a heart with the elegance of a wave. This design is perfect for baristas and coffee enthusiasts looking to add a creative and romantic touch to their coffee presentation. It's a bit more intricate than a standard heart but can be mastered with practice.

Ingredients:

» 1 shot of freshly brewed espresso
» 1 cup of steamed milk with smooth microfoam
» A latte cup (wide and shallow is preferable)
» A milk steaming pitcher

Preparation Time:
5 minutes

Directions:

1. Prepare the Espresso: Brew a shot of espresso directly into your latte cup. Ensure the espresso has a good crema, as it will form the base for your latte art.
2. Steam the Milk: Pour cold milk into a steaming pitcher. Whole milk is often recommended for its ability to create silky microfoam, which is essential for latte art. Steam the milk to achieve a glossy texture, ideally reaching a temperature between 140°F to 150°F (60°C to 65°C).
3. Start Pouring the Milk: Begin by pouring the steamed milk from a height into the center of the espresso. This initial pour integrates the milk with the espresso. As the cup fills halfway, bring the pitcher closer to the surface of the coffee.
4. Create the Heart Shape: Once the pitcher is close to the coffee surface, start pouring more slowly and steadily to create a round blob of foam – this will be the top of your heart.
5. Form the Wave: Without breaking the pour, gently wiggle the pitcher back and forth as you move it away from the initial blob. This motion should be smooth and controlled, creating a rippled, wavy pattern.
6. Complete the Heart: As you reach the bottom of the cup, stop wiggling and drag the milk pour back through the center of your design, pulling through the wave and down to the point of the heart.
7. Serve the coffee as soon as the design is complete to ensure the pattern remains intact and visible.

47 THE APPLE

An imaginative and fun latte art design that adds a whimsical touch to your coffee presentation. It's a creative variation that departs from the more common patterns like hearts and rosettas, perfect for those looking to try something different and playful.

Ingredients:

» 1 shot of freshly brewed espresso
» 1 cup steamed milk with smooth microfoam
» A wide and shallow latte cup - A milk steaming pitcher

Preparation Time:
5 minutes

Directions:

1. Brew the Espresso: Start by brewing a single shot of espresso directly into your latte cup. A good crema on the espresso is essential for a clear and defined latte art design.
2. Steam the Milk: Pour cold milk into a steaming pitcher, with whole milk being preferable for its fat content, which aids in creating a smooth and velvety microfoam. Steam the milk until it reaches a glossy consistency, ideally between 140°F to 150°F (60°C to 65°C).
3. Begin the Pour: Start pouring the steamed milk from a height into the center of the espresso. This initial pouring mixes the milk with the espresso. As the cup fills up, bring the pitcher closer to the surface.
4. Form the Apple Shape: Once the pitcher is close to the coffee surface, start pouring more slowly and steadily to create a round shape - this will be the body of the apple. Pour until the cup is about three-quarters full.
5. Create the Apple's Dip and Stem: To create the dip at the top of the apple, slightly decrease the amount of milk flow and push the pitcher slightly towards one edge of the round shape, then quickly pull back to the center. To make the stem, quickly pour a thin line of milk from the center of the dip upwards towards the edge of the cup.
6. Add a Leaf (Optional): For added detail, you can create a small leaf by pouring a tiny bit of milk at the top of the stem and then using a toothpick or a fine needle to drag out the shape of a leaf.
7. Present the Apple latte art as soon as it's finished to maintain the clarity of the design.

48 THE WREATH

"The Wreath" latte art is a festive and intricate design that resembles a holiday wreath. It's a charming way to add a special touch to your coffee during the holiday season or any time you want to create something unique and eye-catching.

Ingredients:

» 1 shot of freshly brewed espresso
» 1 cup of steamed milk with smooth microfoam
» A wide and shallow latte cup
» A milk steaming pitcher
» A toothpick or a fine needle (for detailing)

Preparation Time:
5 minutes

Directions:

1. Brew the Espresso: Start by brewing a shot of espresso into your latte cup. Ensure the espresso has a consistent crema on top, as this will form the canvas for your latte art.
2. Steam the Milk: Fill a milk pitcher with cold milk. Whole milk is preferred for its creaminess, which is ideal for latte art. Steam the milk until it reaches a silky microfoam texture, ideally between 140°F to 150°F (60°C to 65°C). Aim for microfoam that is integrated well with the milk.
3. Start Pouring the Milk: Begin pouring the steamed milk into the center of the espresso from a height, integrating the milk with the coffee. As the cup fills up halfway, bring the pitcher closer to the surface of the coffee.
4. Create the Wreath Base: Start pouring more slowly and steadily to form a large, round shape in the cup – this will be the base of your wreath. The round should be even and centered.
5. Add Wreath Details: Once your base is formed, use a toothpick or a fine needle to draw small leaf shapes around the circle, mimicking the look of a wreath. You can do this by dragging the tool through the foam to create small indentations that resemble leaves or branches.
6. Final Touches: For an added festive touch, you can create small dots or berry-like shapes along the wreath by carefully dropping tiny amounts of microfoam with the tip of the milk pitcher or a spoon.
7. Present the Wreath latte art as soon as it's completed. This design is best enjoyed fresh to appreciate the intricacies of the pattern.

49 THE BEAR

Creating "The Bear" in latte art is a playful and creative way to add charm to your coffee presentation. This design involves making a bear face, which is not only adorable but also an enjoyable challenge for those looking to expand their latte art skills. While it might seem intricate, with a bit of practice, you can quickly master this delightful design.

Ingredients:

» 1 shot of freshly brewed espresso
» 1 cup of steamed milk with smooth microfoam
» A wide and shallow latte cup
» A milk steaming pitcher
» Cocoa powder (optional, for detailing)
» A small fine brush or toothpick (for detailing)

Preparation Time:
5-7 minutes

Directions:

1. Brew the Espresso: Begin by brewing a single shot of espresso directly into your latte cup. Ensure the espresso has a smooth crema on top, as it serves as the canvas for your latte art.
2. Steam the Milk: Pour cold milk into a steaming pitcher. Whole milk is often recommended for latte art due to its ideal fat content for creating smooth and velvety microfoam. Steam the milk to achieve a glossy texture, ideally reaching a temperature between 140°F to 150°F (60°C to 65°C).
3. Start Pouring the Milk: Begin pouring the steamed milk from a height into the center of the espresso. This initial pouring should mix the milk with the espresso. As the cup fills up halfway, bring the pitcher closer to the surface of the coffee.
4. Form the Bear's Face: Start pouring more slowly and move the pitcher closer to create a large, round blob of foam – this will be the bear's face. Pour until the cup is about three-quarters full.
5. Create the Ears: To make the bear's ears, pour two smaller blobs of foam on either side of the top of the round face. These should be smaller and round, resembling bear ears.
6. Add Facial Details: For the facial details, you can use cocoa powder and a fine brush or toothpick. Gently sprinkle cocoa powder to create the eyes and nose. You can also carefully draw the mouth and other features using the toothpick.
7. Serve Immediately: Once your bear design is complete, serve the coffee immediately to maintain the integrity of the design.

50 THE DRAGON

"The Dragon" latte art is an intricate and impressive design, perfect for those looking to take their coffee presentation to an extraordinary level. This design resembles a mythical dragon and, while challenging, can be achieved with practice and precision. It's an excellent way to showcase advanced latte art skills.

Ingredients:
» 1 shot of freshly brewed espresso
» 1 cup of steamed milk with smooth microfoam
» A wide and shallow latte cup
» A milk steaming pitcher
» Cocoa powder (optional, for detailing)
» A small fine brush or toothpick (for detailing)

Preparation Time:
10 minutes

Directions:
1. Brew the Espresso: Begin by brewing a shot of espresso directly into the latte cup. A smooth and even crema on the espresso is vital as it will be the background for your dragon design.
2. Steam the Milk: Pour cold milk into a steaming pitcher, preferably whole milk for its richness which is ideal for creating velvety microfoam. Steam the milk to achieve a glossy and silky texture, reaching a temperature between 140°F to 150°F (60°C to 65°C).
3. Start Pouring the Milk: Begin pouring the steamed milk from a height into the center of the espresso. This initial pour should mix the milk with the espresso. As the cup fills, bring the pitcher closer to the coffee surface.
4. Form the Dragon's Body: Start pouring more slowly, moving the pitcher in a wavy pattern to create a serpentine shape - this will be the body of the dragon. The motion should be smooth, creating a series of S-shaped curves across the cup.
5. Add the Dragon's Head: At one end of the serpentine shape, pour a small, round blob of foam to form the dragon's head.
6. Detailing the Dragon: Using a fine brush or a toothpick, add details to the dragon's body and head. Use cocoa powder to create the eyes, scales, and other features. This step requires a steady hand and a bit of artistic flair.
7. Complete the Design: Add any final touches to the dragon, such as flames or additional scales, to enhance the overall appearance.
8. Serve Immediately: Once the dragon design is complete, serve the coffee right away. This ensures that the design remains intact and visible for the recipient to enjoy.

51 THE PEACOCK

"The Peacock" latte art is a visually striking design that captures the elegance and beauty of a peacock's tail. This design is a bit more advanced but can be a delightful challenge for those looking to enhance their latte art skills. When perfected, it makes for an incredibly impressive presentation.

Ingredients:

» 1 shot of freshly brewed espresso
» 1 cup of steamed milk with smooth microfoam
» A wide and shallow latte cup
» A milk steaming pitcher
» A toothpick or a fine needle (for detailing)

Preparation Time:
7-10 minutes

Directions:

1. Brew the Espresso: Start by brewing a shot of espresso directly into your latte cup. Ensure that the espresso has a smooth, even crema, which is crucial for a clear latte art design.
2. Steam the Milk: Pour cold milk into a steaming pitcher. Whole milk is often recommended for latte art for its creamy texture, which helps create smooth and velvety microfoam. Steam the milk to a glossy consistency, ideally reaching a temperature between 140°F to 150°F (60°C to 65°C).
3. Start Pouring the Milk: Begin by pouring the steamed milk from a height into the center of the espresso, integrating the milk with the coffee. As the cup fills up halfway, bring the pitcher closer to the surface.
4. Create the Peacock's Body: Pour a large, round blob of foam in the cup's center to form the body of the peacock.
5. Form the Feathers: Start at the top of the blob, pouring a series of small, connected curves or arcs around one side of the blob, creating the impression of the peacock's fanned tail. The motion should be smooth and continuous, creating several loops that get progressively smaller, resembling the pattern of a peacock's feathers.
6. Add Details: Once the basic shape is formed, use a toothpick or a fine needle to add intricate details to the feathers. You can draw lines within each loop to mimic the look of the individual feathers.
7. Final Touches: To complete the peacock design, you can add additional small details like the peacock's head using the toothpick and even small dots to represent the eyes on the feathers.
8. Serve Immediately: Present the completed Peacock latte art as soon as it's finished. This design is best appreciated fresh, showcasing the detailed and artistic effort.

BEYOND THE CUP

5.1 Coffee-Cocktails for Social Hours

52 CLASSIC ESPRESSO MARTINI

A sophisticated and energizing cocktail that combines the rich, bold flavor of coffee with the smoothness of vodka and the sweetness of coffee liqueur. It's a popular choice for an evening out or as a special after-dinner treat.

Ingredients:
» 1 shot of freshly brewed espresso cooled
» 2 ounces of vodka
» 1 ounce of coffee liqueur (such as Kahlúa or Tia Maria)
» ½ ounce of simple syrup (optional, depending on sweetness preference)
» Ice cubes
» Coffee beans (for garnish)

Preparation Time:
5 minutes

Directions:
1. Brew and Cool the Espresso: Begin by brewing a shot of espresso. Allow it to cool to room temperature. You can brew the espresso ahead of time and chill it in the refrigerator for a quicker preparation.
2. Chill the Martini Glass: While the espresso is cooling, place your martini glass in the freezer to chill. This will help keep your cocktail cold and refreshing.
3. Prepare the Cocktail: In a cocktail shaker, combine the cooled espresso, vodka, and coffee liqueur. If you prefer a sweeter cocktail, add simple syrup to taste.
4. Add Ice and Shake: Fill the shaker with ice. Seal it tightly and shake vigorously for about 15-20 seconds. The shaking will chill the cocktail and create a slight froth from the espresso.
5. Strain and Serve: Strain the mixture into the chilled martini glass. The cocktail should have a creamy foam on top from the shaken espresso.
6. Garnish: For a classic presentation, garnish the cocktail by floating three coffee beans on the foam's surface.
7. Enjoy: Serve the Espresso Martini immediately. It's a delightful cocktail that offers a balance of rich coffee flavor with the smoothness of vodka and the sweetness of the liqueur.

53 IRISH COFFEE

A classic and warming cocktail that combines the rich taste of coffee with the smoothness of Irish whiskey, enhanced by the sweetness of sugar and topped with a layer of creamy whipped cream. It's a popular choice for a cozy evening or as a special after-dinner indulgence.

Ingredients:

- » 1 cup of freshly brewed hot coffee
- » 1.5 ounces of irish whiskey
- » 1 to 2 teaspoons of brown sugar (adjust to taste)
- » For topping heavy cream, lightly whipped
- » Grated nutmeg or chocolate (optional, for garnish)

Preparation Time:
10 minutes

Directions:

1. Prepare the Coffee: Start by brewing a strong and rich cup of coffee. Any method of brewing will work, but a French press or a drip coffee maker is commonly used for its robust flavor.
2. Warm the Glass: Preheat your serving glass by filling it with hot water. Let it stand for about a minute and then discard the water. This step ensures that your Irish Coffee stays warm for longer.
3. Add Whiskey and Sugar: Pour the Irish whiskey into the warmed glass. Add the brown sugar. The amount of sugar can be adjusted according to your sweetness preference.
4. Pour in the Coffee: Fill the glass with the freshly brewed hot coffee, leaving about a half-inch at the top for the cream. Stir well until the sugar is completely dissolved in the coffee.
5. Add the Whipped Cream: Gently pour or spoon a thick layer of lightly whipped heavy cream over the back of a spoon onto the coffee. The cream should float on top of the coffee. Do not stir; the coffee is sipped through the layer of cream.
6. Garnish (Optional): For an added touch, you can sprinkle a little grated nutmeg or chocolate over the cream.
7. Serve the Irish Coffee immediately. It's best enjoyed hot, with the warm coffee and whiskey contrasted by the cool cream.

54 COFFEE NEGRONI

A creative twist on the classic Negroni cocktail, introducing the rich and bold flavors of coffee. This variation adds a new dimension to the traditional recipe, combining the bitterness of Campari with the aromatic complexity of coffee. It's perfect for coffee enthusiasts who enjoy a strong and sophisticated cocktail.

Ingredients:

» 1 ounce of gin
» 1 ounce of campari
» 1 ounce of sweet Vermouth
» 1 ounce of cold brew coffee concentrate
» Ice cubes - Orange peel (for garnish)

Preparation Time:
7 minutes

Directions:

1. Gather Ingredients: Have all your ingredients measured and ready. The cold brew coffee concentrate should be strong and rich, which you can prepare in advance by steeping coarsely ground coffee in cold water for about 12-24 hours and then straining.
2. Mix the Cocktail: In a mixing glass, combine the gin, Campari, sweet vermouth, and cold brew coffee concentrate. This cocktail is known for its equal-parts formula, making it straightforward to remember and mix.
3. Stir: Add a handful of ice cubes to the mixing glass. Stir the mixture with a bar spoon for about 30 seconds. This not only chills the drink but also dilutes it slightly, balancing the flavors.
4. Strain the cocktail into an Old Fashioned glass filled with ice. While the traditional Negroni is often served over ice, you can also serve it up in a chilled cocktail glass if preferred.
5. Garnish with a twist of orange peel. To do this, twist the peel over the glass to release the oils and then drop it into the drink or rim the glass with it.
6. Serve the Coffee Negroni immediately. It makes for a great aperitif or a sophisticated after-dinner drink.

55 WHITE RUSSIAN WITH A TWIST

A creamy, indulgent cocktail with an added dimension of flavor that elevates the classic White Russian. This twist on the traditional recipe includes the addition of a unique ingredient or flavor, making it a delightful variation for those who enjoy experimenting with their cocktails.

Ingredients:
» 2 ounces of vodka
» 1 ounce of coffee liqueur (such as Kahlúa)
» 1 ounce of heavy cream
» ½ ounce of cold brew coffee concentrate (for the twist)
» Ice cubes
» Grated chocolate or cocoa powder (optional, for garnish)
» Cinnamon stick (optional, for garnish)

Preparation Time:
5 minutes

Directions:
1. Prepare the Ingredients: Ensure all your ingredients are measured and ready. The cold brew coffee concentrate should be strong and well-chilled, which you can prepare in advance.
2. Combine Vodka and Coffee Liqueur: In an old-fashioned glass, add the vodka and coffee liqueur. This forms the base of your White Russian.
3. Add the Twist - Cold Brew Concentrate: Pour in the cold brew coffee concentrate. This adds an extra layer of rich coffee flavor, enhancing the depth and complexity of the cocktail.
4. Add Ice: Fill the glass with ice cubes, leaving enough room for the cream.
5. Pour in Heavy Cream: Gently pour the heavy cream over the back of a spoon onto the cocktail. This technique allows the cream to sit on top of the alcohol mixture, creating a layered effect.
6. Garnish: For an added touch of elegance, garnish with grated chocolate or a dusting of cocoa powder. You can also add a cinnamon stick for aromatic flair.
7. Serve the White Russian with a Twist immediately. The drink can be stirred before drinking to mix the layers or sipped as is to enjoy the contrast between the creamy top and the coffee-flavored base.

56 COFFEE OLD FASHIONED

A sophisticated and robust cocktail that combines the classic elements of an Old Fashioned with the rich, deep flavors of coffee. This modern twist on the traditional whiskey cocktail is perfect for those who appreciate the complexity of a good bourbon coupled with the aromatic nuances of coffee.

Ingredients:

» 2 ounces of bourbon or rye whiskey
» ½ ounce of cold brew coffee concentrate
» ½ ounce of simple syrup
» 2 dashes of angostura bitters
» For garnish: orange peel
» Ice cubes
» Coffee beans (optional, for garnish)

Preparation Time:
5 minutes

Directions:

1. Prepare Ingredients: Ensure your cold brew coffee concentrate is prepared in advance. It should be strong and chilled to enhance the cocktail's flavor profile.
2. Combine Whiskey, Coffee Concentrate, and Simple Syrup: In a mixing glass, add the bourbon or rye whiskey, cold brew coffee concentrate, and simple syrup. The simple syrup adds a touch of sweetness to balance the bitterness of the coffee and the whiskey.
3. Add Bitters: Incorporate two dashes of Angostura bitters. This classic cocktail ingredient adds depth and complexity to the drink.
4. Stir the Cocktail: Fill the mixing glass with ice and stir the mixture for about 30 seconds. This chills the cocktail and dilutes it slightly, mellowing the flavors and ensuring a smooth sip.
5. Strain into Glass: Strain the cocktail into an Old Fashioned glass filled with ice. Using a large ice cube or sphere is traditional and ensures slower melting, keeping the drink colder for longer without excessive dilution.
6. Garnish: Express the oils of an orange peel over the drink by gently twisting it above the glass, then rim the glass with the peel to impart the aroma. Drop the peel into the drink as a garnish. For an added touch, you can also garnish with a few coffee beans.
7. Serve the Coffee Old Fashioned immediately. This cocktail is perfect as an evening sipper or a sophisticated after-dinner drink.

57 MEXICAN COFFEE

A rich and flavorful beverage that combines the boldness of coffee with the unique sweetness of piloncillo (unrefined cane sugar) and the warmth of Mexican spices. It's a traditional drink that offers a delightful twist on regular coffee, perfect for those who enjoy a spiced and slightly sweet coffee experience.

Ingredients:

» 1 cup of freshly brewed hot coffee
» 1 to 2 tablespoons of piloncillo (or dark brown sugar as a substitute) (adjust to taste)
» 1 cinnamon stick
» A pinch of ground cloves
» A pinch of ground nutmeg
» 1 ounce of chocolate (preferably Mexican chocolate) chopped or grated
» ½ teaspoon of vanilla extract
» Whipped cream (optional, for topping)
» Ground cinnamon (optional, for garnish)

Preparation Time:
10 minutes

Directions:

1. Brew the Coffee: Begin by brewing your coffee. You can use any brewing method you prefer, but a medium to dark roast coffee works best for this recipe to complement the rich flavors of the additional ingredients.
2. Prepare the Piloncillo Mixture: In a small saucepan, combine the piloncillo (or dark brown sugar), cinnamon stick, ground cloves, and ground nutmeg. Add a small amount of water (about ¼ cup) to help dissolve the piloncillo and blend the spices.
3. Simmer: Heat the mixture over medium heat, stirring constantly until the piloncillo is fully dissolved and the mixture is fragrant. This will take about 3-5 minutes.
4. Add Chocolate and Vanilla: Once the piloncillo has dissolved, add the chopped or grated chocolate and vanilla extract to the saucepan. Stir until the chocolate is completely melted and the mixture is smooth.
5. Combine with Coffee: Pour the freshly brewed hot coffee into the saucepan with the spiced piloncillo and chocolate mixture. Stir well to ensure all the ingredients are thoroughly combined.
6. Serve: Pour the Mexican coffee into a cup or mug. Top with whipped cream if desired, and sprinkle a little ground cinnamon on top for garnish.
7. Enjoy your Mexican Coffee, a warm and spiced beverage that's perfect for a cozy morning or as a special after-dinner treat.

58 MINT COFFEE COCKTAIL

A refreshing and invigorating drink that blends the rich flavors of coffee with the cool, crisp taste of mint. This cocktail is perfect for those who enjoy a hint of freshness in their coffee, making it an excellent choice for a summer evening or a special occasion.

Ingredients:

Preparation Time:
5 minutes

» 1 shot of freshly brewed espresso or strong coffee
» 1 ounce of crème de menthe (green)
» 1 ounce of vodka
» ½ ounce of simple syrup (adjust to taste)
» Ice cubes
» For garnish: fresh mint leaves
» Coffee beans (optional, for garnish)

Directions:

1. Brew the Espresso/Coffee: Begin by brewing a shot of espresso or strong coffee. Allow it to cool slightly. If you prefer a colder cocktail, you can brew the coffee ahead of time and chill it in the refrigerator.
2. Combine Ingredients: In a cocktail shaker, combine the cooled espresso or coffee, crème de menthe, vodka, and simple syrup. The simple syrup can be adjusted according to how sweet you like your cocktail.
3. Add Ice and Shake: Fill the shaker with ice. Seal it tightly and shake vigorously for about 15-20 seconds. Shaking not only chills the drink but also helps to blend the flavors thoroughly.
4. Strain and Serve: Strain the mixture into a chilled cocktail glass. A martini glass works well for this cocktail.
5. Garnish with fresh mint leaves. For an added touch of sophistication, you can also garnish with a few coffee beans.
6. Enjoy: Serve the Mint Coffee Cocktail immediately. It's a delightful and refreshing cocktail that offers a balance of rich coffee flavor with the cooling sensation of mint.

59 BRANDY COFFEE ALEXANDER

A luxurious and creamy cocktail that combines the rich flavors of coffee with the warmth of brandy, accented by the sweetness of crème de cacao. This indulgent drink is a variation of the classic Brandy Alexander, making it an excellent choice for those who enjoy a coffee-infused twist on traditional cocktails.

Ingredients:

» 1 ounce of brandy
» 1 ounce of dark crème de cacao
» 1 ounce of freshly brewed espresso or strong coffee cooled
» 1 ounce of heavy cream
» Ice cubes
» Ground nutmeg or cinnamon (optional, for garnish)
» Whipped cream (optional, for topping)

Preparation Time:
7 minutes

Directions:

1. Brew Espresso/Coffee: Begin by brewing a shot of espresso or strong coffee. Allow it to cool to room temperature. For a colder cocktail, you can brew the coffee ahead of time and refrigerate it.
2. Combine Ingredients in a Shaker: In a cocktail shaker, add the brandy, dark crème de cacao, cooled espresso or coffee, and heavy cream. These ingredients create a rich and balanced base for the cocktail
3. Shake with Ice: Add a handful of ice cubes to the shaker. Seal the shaker tightly and shake vigorously for about 20 seconds. This process will chill the cocktail and create a slightly frothy texture.
4. Strain into a Glass: Strain the mixture into a chilled cocktail glass, such as a martini or coupe glass. The cocktail should have a smooth and creamy consistency.
5. Garnish the Brandy Coffee Alexander with a light sprinkle of ground nutmeg or cinnamon on top. For an extra touch of indulgence, you can top it with a dollop of whipped cream.
6. Enjoy: Serve the cocktail immediately. The Brandy Coffee Alexander is a delightful and sophisticated drink, perfect as an after-dinner treat or for special occasions.

60 AMARETTO COFFEE COCKTAIL

A warm, soothing beverage that beautifully combines the rich, nutty flavor of amaretto with the boldness of coffee. It's a delightful after-dinner drink that offers a sweet and comforting experience, perfect for sipping on a relaxed evening or after a meal.

Ingredients:
» 1 cup of freshly brewed hot coffee
» 1.5 ounces of amaretto liqueur
» For topping: Whipped cream
» Ground cinnamon or chocolate shavings (optional, for garnish)
» Brown sugar or sweetener (optional, to taste)

Preparation Time:
5 minutes

Directions:
1. Brew the Coffee: Start by brewing your favorite coffee. A medium or dark roast works well in this recipe as it complements the sweetness of the amaretto.
2. Sweeten the Coffee (Optional): If you prefer your coffee with a bit of added sweetness, stir in some brown sugar or your preferred sweetener to the hot coffee until it's dissolved.
3. Add Amaretto: Pour the amaretto liqueur into the cup of hot coffee. Stir gently to combine the flavors.
4. Top with Whipped Cream: Add a generous dollop of whipped cream on top of the coffee. The cream not only adds a luxurious texture but also balances the strong flavors of the coffee and amaretto.
5. Garnish: Sprinkle a pinch of ground cinnamon or chocolate shavings over the whipped cream for an added touch of flavor and an elegant presentation.
6. Serve the Amaretto Coffee Cocktail immediately, while it's still warm and the whipped cream is fluffy.

61 CINNAMON ROLL COFFEE COCKTAIL

A delightful, dessert-like drink that beautifully marries the flavors of a warm cinnamon roll with a comforting coffee cocktail. This indulgent beverage is perfect for those who enjoy the sweet, spicy essence of cinnamon paired with the rich depth of coffee and the smoothness of liqueur.

Ingredients:
» 1 cup of freshly brewed hot coffee
» 1 ounce of cinnamon liqueur (such as Fireball Whisky)
» 1 ounce of irish cream liqueur (such as Baileys)
» ½ ounce of vanilla vodka
» For topping: whipped cream
» For garnish: ground cinnamon
» Cinnamon stick (optional, for garnish)

Preparation Time:
7 minutes

Directions:
1. Brew the Coffee: Start by brewing a strong and rich cup of coffee. A medium or dark roast coffee is ideal for this cocktail as it complements the other flavors.
2. Add the Liqueurs and Vodka: Pour the cinnamon liqueur, Irish cream liqueur, and vanilla vodka into the hot coffee. Stir gently to combine the ingredients evenly. The cinnamon liqueur brings in the spicy sweetness reminiscent of a cinnamon roll, while the Irish cream and vanilla vodka add creamy and smooth undertones.
3. Top with Whipped Cream: Add a generous layer of whipped cream on top of the cocktail. The whipped cream mimics the frosting on a cinnamon roll and adds a creamy texture to the drink.
4. Garnish: Sprinkle a pinch of ground cinnamon over the whipped cream for an extra hint of spice. For an added decorative touch, you can also add a cinnamon stick as a stirrer.
5. Serve the Cinnamon Roll Coffee Cocktail immediately. It's best enjoyed warm, allowing all the flavors to meld together beautifully.

5.2 Coffee-Infused Bites: Snacks for a Quick Coffee Fix

62 COFFEE CHOCOLATE ENERGY BALLS

A lovely and energizing snack, perfect for those needing a quick coffee fix combined with the richness of chocolate. These no-bake treats are packed with natural ingredients, offering a healthier alternative to conventional snacks while still providing a boost of energy.

Preparation Time:
20 minutes

Ingredients:
» 1 cup of medjool dates pitted
» ½ cup of raw almonds
» ½ cup of rolled oats
» ¼ cup of unsweetened cocoa powder
» 2 tablespoons of ground coffee or espresso powder
» 2 tablespoons of honey or maple syrup
» 1 teaspoon of vanilla extract
» A pinch of sea salt
» Optional: Shredded coconut, cocoa powder, or crushed nuts for coating

Directions:
1. Prepare the Ingredients: Ensure that the Medjool dates are pitted. If they are too dry, soak them in warm water for about 10 minutes, then drain. Measure out the almonds, oats, cocoa powder, and coffee.
2. Blend the Ingredients: In a food processor, add the pitted Medjool dates, raw almonds, and rolled oats. Process them until they form a coarse mixture. Add the cocoa powder, ground coffee or espresso powder, honey or maple syrup, vanilla extract, and a pinch of sea salt. Blend again until the mixture starts to come together and forms a sticky dough. If the mixture is too dry, you can add a little more honey or syrup.
3. Form the Energy Balls: Take small portions of the mixture and roll them into balls using your hands. The size can vary, but typically they should be about the size of a walnut. If the mixture is sticking to your hands, wetting them slightly can help
4. Coat the Energy Balls (Optional): Roll the energy balls in shredded coconut, extra cocoa powder, or crushed nuts for an additional flavor and texture. This step is optional but adds to the visual appeal and taste.
5. Chill and Set: Place the energy balls on a baking sheet lined with parchment paper. Refrigerate for about 10-15 minutes to allow them to set and firm up.
6. Serve: Once set, the Coffee Chocolate Energy Balls are ready to be served. They can be enjoyed as a quick snack, a post workout energy boost, or a healthier dessert option.
7. Storage: Store any leftover energy balls in an airtight container in the refrigerator for up to a week, or in the freezer for longer storage.

63 MOCHA PROTEIN BARS

A fantastic snack for coffee lovers and fitness enthusiasts alike. Combining the rich flavors of coffee and chocolate with the benefits of protein, these bars are perfect for a pre-workout boost, a post-exercise snack, or simply for those times when you need an energizing pick-me-up.

Ingredients:

» 1 cup of rolled oats
» 1 cup of whey or plant-based protein powder (chocolate or vanilla flavor)
» ¼ cup of unsweetened cocoa powder
» 2 tablespoons of ground espresso or coffee
» ½ cup of almond butter or peanut butter
» ⅓ cup of honey or maple syrup
» 1 teaspoon of vanilla extract
» About ¼ cup of almond milk (or any milk of choice) as needed
» ½ cup of dark chocolate chips (optional)
» A pinch of salt

Preparation Time:
20 minutes
(plus chilling time)

Directions:

1. Prepare Dry Ingredients: In a large mixing bowl, combine the rolled oats, protein powder, cocoa powder, ground espresso, and a pinch of salt. Mix well to ensure that all ingredients are evenly distributed.
2. Mix in Wet Ingredients: Add almond butter (or peanut butter) and honey (or maple syrup) to the mixture. Pour in the vanilla extract. Stir the mixture thoroughly until it starts to come together. It should have a sticky, dough-like consistency. If the mixture is too dry, gradually add almond milk (or your choice of milk) to reach the desired consistency.
3. Add Chocolate Chips (Optional): If using, fold in the dark chocolate chips into the mixture for added sweetness and texture.
4. Form the Bars: Line a baking dish or tray with parchment paper. Transfer the mixture to the prepared dish. Press down firmly and evenly to form a compact, even layer. You can use the back of a spoon or your hands to press the mixture into the dish.
5. Chill and Set: Refrigerate the tray for at least 1-2 hours to allow the bars to set and firm up.
6. Cut into Bars: Once chilled and set, remove the mixture from the tray and cut it into bars or squares. The size of the bars can be adjusted according to your preference.
7. Serve or Store: The Mocha Protein Bars are now ready to be served. They can be enjoyed as a convenient and satisfying snack. Store any leftover bars in an airtight container in the refrigerator for up to a week, or freeze them for longer storage.

64 COFFEE-INFUSED OATMEAL

An energizing and nutritious breakfast option, combining the rich, robust flavor of coffee with the wholesomeness of oatmeal. This dish is perfect for coffee lovers looking to kickstart their morning with a caffeine boost and a hearty meal.

Ingredients:
» 1 cup of rolled oats
» 1 cup of brewed coffee (preferably strong coffee)
» 1 cup of water
» A pinch of salt
» ½ cup of milk or a milk alternative (optional, for creaminess)
» To taste brown sugar, honey, or maple syrup (optional, for sweetness)
» ½ teaspoon of vanilla extract
» ½ teaspoon of ground cinnamon (optional)
» Toppings: Fresh fruits, nuts, seeds, chocolate chips, or a dollop of yogurt

Preparation Time:
15-20 minutes

Directions:
1. Brew the Coffee: Prepare 1 cup of strong brewed coffee using your preferred method. A rich and robust coffee works best for infusing the oatmeal with a distinct coffee flavor.
2. Combine Coffee and Oats: In a medium-sized saucepan, combine the rolled oats, brewed coffee, and water. Add a pinch of salt to enhance the flavors.
3. Cook the Oatmeal: Place the saucepan over medium heat. Bring the mixture to a boil, then reduce the heat to a simmer. Stir the oatmeal frequently to prevent it from sticking to the bottom of the pan. Cook for about 5-10 minutes, or until the oats are soft and have absorbed most of the liquid. The cooking time may vary depending on the type of oats used.
4. Add Creaminess and Flavor: For a creamier texture, stir in the milk or milk alternative. Add brown sugar, honey, or maple syrup to sweeten the oatmeal to your liking. Stir in the vanilla extract and ground cinnamon (if using) for added flavor.
5. Serve with Toppings: Once the oatmeal is cooked to your desired consistency, remove it from the heat. Serve the coffee-infused oatmeal in bowls. Top with your choice of fresh fruits, nuts, seeds, chocolate chips, or a dollop of yogurt. These toppings add texture, nutrition, and extra flavor to the oatmeal.
6. Enjoy your Coffee-Infused Oatmeal warm, perfect for a cozy and energizing start to your day.

65 ESPRESSO BEAN TRAIL MIX

An energizing and tasty snack perfect for coffee enthusiasts and those needing a quick pick-me-up. This trail mix combines the rich flavor of espresso beans with a variety of nuts and dried fruits, offering a balance of textures and flavors that are both satisfying and invigorating.

Ingredients:

Preparation Time:
10 minutes

» Dark chocolate
» 1 cup of covered espresso beans
» ½ cup of raw almonds
» ½ cup of walnuts
» ½ cup of dried cranberries or cherries
» ¼ cup of pumpkin seeds (pepitas)
» ¼ cup of dried coconut flakes
» A pinch of sea salt
» Optional: dark chocolate chips, banana chips, or any other preferred nuts or dried fruits

Directions:

1. Gather and Prepare Ingredients: Ensure that all ingredients are ready to use. If you prefer smaller pieces, roughly chop the nuts to make them more uniform in size with the espresso beans and dried fruits.
2. Mix the Ingredients: In a large mixing bowl, combine the dark chocolate-covered espresso beans, raw almonds, walnuts, dried cranberries or cherries, pumpkin seeds, and dried coconut flakes. If adding other ingredients like dark chocolate chips or banana chips, mix them in at this stage. Sprinkle a pinch of sea salt over the mixture and toss well to ensure even distribution.
3. Store the Trail Mix: Transfer the trail mix into an airtight container or divide it into individual snack-sized bags for convenience. Storing the trail mix in a cool, dry place will help maintain its freshness and crunch.
4. Serve and Enjoy: Your Espresso Bean Trail Mix is now ready to be enjoyed. It's perfect as a mid-morning snack, a quick energy booster during hikes or long drives, or even as a tasty topping for yogurts and oatmeal.
5. Optional Additions and Variations: Feel free to customize the trail mix according to your taste preferences. You can add other ingredients like cashews, pecans, or sunflower seeds. For a sweeter mix, consider adding mini marshmallows or chunks of dried fruit like mangoes or apricots. For a spicy twist, add a dash of cinnamon or cayenne pepper.

66 COFFEE BANANA SMOOTHIE

A refreshing and energizing drink, perfect for those mornings when you need an extra boost. This smoothie combines the rich taste of coffee with the natural sweetness of bananas, along with a few other ingredients to create a delicious and nutritious beverage.

Ingredients:
» 1 cup of brewed coffee cooled or chilled
» 1 ripe banana preferably frozen
» ½ cup of greek yogurt or a dairy-free alternative
» 1 tablespoon of honey or maple syrup (adjust to taste)
» ½ teaspoon of vanilla extract
» ¼ teaspoon of ground cinnamon
» A handful ice cubes
» Optional: a scoop of protein powder (vanilla or unflavored)

Preparation Time:
5-10 minutes

Directions:
1. Prepare the Coffee: Brew a cup of your favorite coffee and allow it to cool. For a quicker option, you can use instant coffee dissolved in hot water. Once brewed, place it in the refrigerator to chill. Using cold coffee helps to keep the smoothie chilled and refreshing.
2. Prep the Banana If you haven't already, peel and slice a ripe banana, then freeze it. Frozen bananas give the smoothie a creamy texture and a cold temperature.
3. Blend the Ingredients: In a blender, combine the chilled coffee, frozen banana, Greek yogurt, honey or maple syrup, vanilla extract, and ground cinnamon. If you're including protein powder, add it to the blender at this stage.
4. Add Ice and Blend: Add a handful of ice cubes to the blender. Blend all the ingredients until smooth and creamy. If the smoothie is too thick, you can add a little more coffee or water to reach your desired consistency.
5. Taste and Adjust: Taste the smoothie and adjust the sweetness if necessary. Depending on the ripeness of the banana and your personal preference, you might want to add more honey or maple syrup.
6. Serve: Pour the smoothie into a glass and serve immediately. For an added touch, you can sprinkle a little more cinnamon on top or garnish with a few coffee beans.
7. Enjoy your Coffee Banana Smoothie as a quick breakfast, a post-workout drink, or as a midday pick-me-up.

67 COFFEE-FLAVORED YOGURT PARFAIT

An elegant dessert or breakfast option that combines the rich taste of coffee with the creamy texture of yogurt. Layered with granola and fruits, it offers a perfect balance of flavors and textures. This dish is ideal for coffee enthusiasts who enjoy a hint of coffee in their sweet treats.

Ingredients:
- » 2 cups of greek yogurt or a dairy-free alternative
- » 1-2 tablespoons of instant coffee powder or espresso powder (adjust according to strength preference)
- » 2 tablespoons of honey or maple syrup (adjust to taste)
- » 1 teaspoon of vanilla extract
- » 1 cup of granola (choose your favorite variety)
- » 1 cup of fresh fruits (like berries, sliced bananas, or kiwi)
- » Optional toppings: Chopped nuts, chocolate shavings, or a sprinkle of cinnamon

Preparation Time:
15 minutes

Directions:
1. Prepare the Coffee-Flavored Yogurt: In a medium-sized mixing bowl, combine the Greek yogurt with the instant coffee or espresso powder. Stir well until the coffee is completely dissolved and the mixture is uniform in color. This will create your coffee-flavored yogurt base. Add honey or maple syrup and vanilla extract to the yogurt. Mix well until all the ingredients are fully incorporated and the yogurt is sweetened to your liking.
2. Layer the Parfait: Take two glasses or parfait cups. Begin by adding a layer of granola at the bottom of each cup. Follow this with a layer of the coffee-flavored yogurt. Add a layer of fresh fruits on top of the yogurt. Repeat these layers until the glasses are filled to the top, finishing with a layer of fruits.
3. Add Toppings (Optional): For added crunch and flavor, sprinkle chopped nuts, chocolate shavings, or a dash of cinnamon on top of the parfait. You can customize the toppings based on your preference or dietary needs.
4. Chill (Optional): If preferred, you can chill the parfaits in the refrigerator for about 30 minutes before serving. This step is optional but can enhance the flavors and make the parfait more refreshing.
5. Serve the Coffee-Flavored Yogurt Parfait immediately if not chilled. If you have refrigerated the parfaits, take them out just before serving
6. Enjoy this delightful parfait as a luxurious breakfast, a midday snack, or as a dessert. It's a perfect combination of health and flavor, suitable for any time of the day.

68 COFFEE GLAZED NUTS

Coffee Glazed Nuts are a delightful snack that combines the rich, aromatic flavor of coffee with the crunchy goodness of nuts. This treat is perfect for coffee lovers and is an excellent snack for parties, a quick pick-me-up during the day, or as a unique gift.

Ingredients:

»   2 cups of mixed nuts (such as almonds, walnuts, pecans, and cashews)
»   ¼ cup of strong brewed coffee
»   ½ cup of brown sugar
»   1 teaspoon of vanilla extract
»   ½ teaspoon of ground cinnamon
»   A pinch salt
»   Optional: A pinch of cayenne pepper for a spicy kick

Preparation Time:
30 minutes

Directions:

1. Preheat the Oven and Prepare the Baking Sheet: Preheat your oven to 350°F (175°C). Line a baking sheet with parchment paper or a silicone baking mat. This will prevent the nuts from sticking and make clean-up easier.
2. Toast the Nuts: Spread the nuts in a single layer on the prepared baking sheet. Toast them in the preheated oven for about 10 minutes, stirring once halfway through, until they are lightly browned and fragrant. Be careful not to burn them. Remove the nuts from the oven and set aside.
3. Prepare the Coffee Glaze: In a small saucepan, combine the brewed coffee and brown sugar. Stir over medium heat until the sugar is completely dissolved. Bring the mixture to a simmer and let it reduce slightly for about 5 minutes until it thickens. Remove from heat and stir in the vanilla extract, ground cinnamon, salt, and cayenne pepper (if using).
4. Coat the Nuts: Pour the coffee glaze over the toasted nuts. Gently toss until all the nuts are evenly coated with the glaze.
5. Bake the Glazed Nuts: Spread the glazed nuts back onto the baking sheet in a single layer. Bake in the oven for about 10-15 minutes, stirring occasionally, until the nuts are glazed and slightly crispy. Watch closely in the last few minutes to prevent burning.
6. Cool and Serve: Remove the nuts from the oven and let them cool completely on the baking sheet. As they cool, the glaze will harden and become crunchy. Once cooled, break apart any large clumps of nuts.
7. Enjoy: Your Coffee Glazed Nuts are ready to be enjoyed! Serve them as a snack or package them in jars or bags for a delightful homemade gift.

69 COFFEE AND OAT BREAKFAST COOKIES

Coffee and Oat Breakfast Cookies are a lovely and nutritious way to start your day, especially for those who love the flavor of coffee. These cookies combine the energizing effect of coffee with the wholesomeness of oats, nuts, and fruits, making them a perfect grab-and-go breakfast or snack.

Ingredients:

» 2 tablespoons of instant coffee granules
» 1 tablespoon of hot water
» 1 ½ cups of rolled oats
» ½ cup of whole wheat flour or all-purpose flour
» 1 teaspoon of baking powder
» ½ teaspoon of ground cinnamon
» ¼ teaspoon of salt
» ½ cup of unsalted butter, softened
» ⅓ cup of brown sugar
» 1 large egg
» 1 teaspoon of vanilla extract
» ½ cup of raisins or dried cranberries
» ½ cup of chopped walnuts or almonds
» Optional: ½ cup of dark chocolate chips

Preparation Time:
35 minutes

Directions:

1. Preheat the Oven and Prepare the Baking Sheet: Preheat your oven to 350°F (175°C). Line a baking sheet with parchment paper or lightly grease it.
2. Dissolve the Coffee: In a small bowl, dissolve the instant coffee granules in 1 tablespoon of hot water. Set aside to cool slightly.
3. Mix Dry Ingredients: In a medium bowl, combine the rolled oats, flour, baking powder, ground cinnamon, and salt. Mix well and set aside.
4. Cream Butter and Sugar: In a large bowl, use an electric mixer to cream the softened butter and brown sugar together until light and fluffy. Beat in the egg, followed by the vanilla extract and the coffee mixture. Mix until well incorporated
5. Combine Wet and Dry Ingredients: Gradually add the dry oat mixture to the wet ingredients, stirring just until combined.
6. Add Fruits, Nuts, and Chocolate (Optional): Fold in the raisins or dried cranberries and chopped nuts. If using, also add the dark chocolate chips.
7. Shape and Bake the Cookies: Drop tablespoon-sized portions of the cookie dough onto the prepared baking sheet, spacing them about 2 inches apart. Flatten the cookies slightly with the back of the spoon or your fingers. Bake in the preheated oven for 12-15 minutes or until the edges are golden brown.
8. Cool the Cookies: Remove the cookies from the oven and allow them to cool on the baking sheet for a few minutes. Transfer to a wire rack to cool completely.
9. Serve and Enjoy: Your Coffee and Oat Breakfast Cookies are ready to be enjoyed! They can be served warm or stored in an airtight container for later consumption.

COFFEE FOR EVERY OCCASION

6.1 Coffee for One: Solo Recipes for Personal Enjoyment

70 SINGLE-SERVE FRENCH PRESS COFFEE

An ideal way to make a rich and full-bodied cup of coffee. This method allows the coffee grounds to fully steep in the water, extracting deep flavors and essential oils.

Ingredients:

» Fresh coffee beans: approximately 2 tablespoons
» 1 cup of hot water just off the boil
» A single-serve French press (typically around 12-17 ounces in size)

Preparation Time:
10 minutes

Directions:

1. Grind the Coffee Beans: Begin by grinding your coffee beans to a coarse consistency, akin to breadcrumbs. This grind size is perfect for French press brewing as it prevents the grounds from slipping through the press's filter.
2. Heat the French Press: Preheat your French press by rinsing it with hot water. This step warms up the press, ensuring your coffee stays hot during the brewing process.
3. Add Coffee Grounds to French Press: Discard the rinse water and add your freshly ground coffee to the press.
4. Add Hot Water: Pour hot water just off the boil over the grounds, filling up to the desired level of your French press. Make sure to saturate all the grounds evenly.
5. Stir Gently: Give the grounds a gentle stir with a spoon to ensure they are fully immersed in the water. This helps in even extraction of the coffee flavors.
6. Let the Coffee Brew: Place the lid on the French press with the plunger pulled all the way up. Allow the coffee to brew for about 4 minutes. This duration is ideal for a balanced extraction.
7. Plunge: After 4 minutes, slowly and steadily press the plunger down. If you find resistance while plunging, your coffee may be ground too fine; if it plunges too easily, the grind may be too coarse.
8. Serve Immediately: pour your freshly brewed coffee into a cup. Allowing the coffee to sit in the French press can result in over-extraction and bitterness.

71 PERFECT POUR-OVER COFFEE

Pour-over coffee is a method that brings out intricate flavors and aromas in coffee, offering a clean and complex cup. It requires precision and patience but rewards you with an exceptional coffee experience. This recipe outlines how to make a perfect pour-over coffee.

Ingredients:

» Fresh coffee beans: about 3 tablespoons
» Filtered water: about 13.5 ounces
» A pour-over coffee maker (like a Chemex, Hario V60, or similar)
» A paper filter (appropriate to your device)
» A kettle (preferably a gooseneck kettle for better control)
» A coffee grinder
» A scale (optional but recommended)
» A timer

Preparation Time:
12 minutes

Directions:

1. Heat the Water: Begin by heating your water to about 195°F to 205°F (90°C to 96°C). Using a gooseneck kettle will give you more control over the pouring process. If you don't have a thermometer, bring the water to a boil and then let it sit for about 30 seconds to cool slightly.
2. Grind the Coffee: While your water is heating, grind the coffee beans to a medium-fine consistency, similar to sea salt. The grind should not be too fine or too coarse; it should feel like granulated sugar.
3. Prepare the Pour-Over and Filter: Place your pour-over device on your cup or carafe. Insert the paper filter and rinse it with hot water to eliminate any paper taste and to preheat the pour-over and cup. Discard the rinse water.
4. Add Coffee Grounds: Place your ground coffee into the filter. If using a scale, make sure it's tared to zero with the pour-over and filter on it.
5. Bloom the Coffee: Start your timer and pour enough water (about 50 ml) to saturate all the coffee grounds evenly. This process allows the coffee to de-gas, enabling better extraction. Let it sit for about 30 seconds.
6. Begin Pouring: After the bloom, continue pouring the water in a slow and steady spiral, starting from the center and moving outwards, and then back towards the center. The goal is to keep the water level consistent for an even extraction.
7. Control the Pour: Continue to pour slowly, maintaining a gentle and steady pace. The entire pouring process should take about 2 to 2.5 minutes.
8. Finish Brewing: Once you've poured all the water, let the coffee continue to drip until the dripping slows to a stop. This should take about 30 seconds to 1 minute.
9. Remove the Pour-Over and Serve: Discard the grounds and filter. Serve the coffee immediately for the best flavor.

72 SPICED SOLO MOCHA

A delightful and warming beverage that combines the richness of chocolate with the deep flavors of coffee and the aromatic essence of spices. It's a single-serve treat perfect for cozy moments or when you need a comforting, spiced coffee experience.

Ingredients:

» 1 shot of freshly brewed espresso or strong coffee
» ¾ cup of milk
» 2 tablespoons of dark chocolate chopped or in chip form
» ¼ teaspoon of cinnamon powder
» A pinch of nutmeg powder
» A few drops of vanilla extract
» Brown sugar or sweetener of choice: to taste (optional)
» Whipped cream (optional, for topping)
» Additional cinnamon or chocolate shavings (optional, for garnish)
» Optional toppings: Chopped nuts, chocolate shavings, or a sprinkle of cinnamon

Preparation Time:
10 minutes

Directions:

1. Brew the Espresso/Coffee: Begin by brewing a shot of espresso or making a small, strong cup of coffee. The strength and quality of the coffee are essential as it forms the base of your mocha.
2. Heat and Spice the Milk: In a saucepan, heat the milk over medium heat. Do not boil. Once the milk is hot, add the cinnamon and nutmeg, stirring well to incorporate. These spices will give your mocha a warm, aromatic flavor.
3. Melt the Chocolate: Add the dark chocolate to the hot, spiced milk. Stir continuously until the chocolate is completely melted and the mixture is smooth. For a sweeter mocha, you can add brown sugar or your preferred sweetener.
4. Add Vanilla Extract: Stir in a few drops of vanilla extract for an added layer of flavor.
5. Combine with Coffee: Pour the freshly brewed espresso or coffee into a large mug. Then, add the spiced chocolate milk mixture. Stir well to ensure all the ingredients are evenly mixed.
6. Top with Whipped Cream: If desired, top your mocha with a dollop of whipped cream for a creamy, luxurious finish.
7. Garnish: Sprinkle a bit of cinnamon or chocolate shavings on top of the whipped cream for an extra touch of spice and elegance.
8. Serve: Enjoy your Spiced Solo Mocha immediately. It's perfect for savoring slowly on a chilly day or whenever you crave a spiced, chocolatey coffee treat.

73 CLASSIC DALGONA COFFEE

Dalgona Coffee, a beverage that gained popularity on social media, is known for its creamy whipped coffee topping over milk. Originating from South Korea, it's a visually stunning and deliciously rich drink. Making Dalgona Coffee is simple and requires only a few ingredients.

Ingredients:

» 2 tablespoons of instant coffee powder
» 2 tablespoons of granulated sugar
» 2 tablespoons of hot water
» 2/3 cups of milk approximately cold or hot (based on preference)
» Ice cubes (optional, for serving with cold milk)

Preparation Time:
15 minutes

Directions:

1. Prepare the Whipped Coffee Mixture: In a mixing bowl, combine the instant coffee powder, granulated sugar, and hot water. The equal ratio is crucial for achieving the right texture and sweetness. Using a hand mixer or a whisk, vigorously whisk the mixture. You can also use a fork or a hand whisk, but it will require more effort and time. - Continue whisking until the mixture becomes light, fluffy, and holds stiff peaks. This process typically takes about 5 to 10 minutes, depending on the tools used. The mixture should have a creamy, whipped texture similar to that of whipped cream.

2. Prepare the Milk: If you prefer cold Dalgona Coffee, fill a glass about three-quarters full with cold milk and add a few ice cubes. For a hot version, heat the milk and pour it into a mug, filling it three-quarters of the way. The choice of milk can vary based on dietary preferences. Regular dairy milk, almond milk, soy milk, or other alternatives work well with this recipe.

3. Assemble the Dalgona Coffee: With a spoon, carefully dollop the whipped coffee mixture on top of the prepared milk. Gently smooth the top for an even layer, or create a peak for a more dramatic presentation. For an added touch, you can sprinkle a bit of cocoa powder, coffee powder, or a drizzle of caramel or chocolate syrup on top.

4. Serve the Dalgona Coffee with a long spoon or straw. Mix the whipped coffee with the milk before drinking to enjoy the full flavor. The drink is best enjoyed immediately after preparation to savor the contrast between the creamy whipped coffee and the milk.

74 ESPRESSO CON PANNA

Espresso Con Panna, which means "espresso with cream" in Italian, is a classic coffee drink that combines the intensity of espresso with the richness of whipped cream. This simple yet luxurious beverage is perfect for those who appreciate the robust flavor of espresso but also enjoy a touch of creamy sweetness.

Ingredients:

» Freshly ground espresso beans: enough for 1 shot
» Heavy cream: about ¼ cup
» Sugar or sweetener (optional, for the cream)
» Cocoa powder or chocolate shavings (optional, for garnish)

Preparation Time:
8 minutes

Directions:

1. Brew the Espresso: Start by grinding your espresso beans to a fine consistency. The grind should be suitable for espresso, finer than what you would use for regular drip coffee. Using an espresso machine, brew one shot (about 30 ml) of espresso. Ensure that your espresso machine is properly heated and the portafilter is evenly tamped for the best extraction. Pour the freshly brewed espresso into a small, clear espresso cup or a demitasse to showcase the layers of the drink.

2. Whip the Cream: In a bowl, pour the heavy cream. You can add a bit of sugar or sweetener if you prefer a slightly sweetened cream. However, traditionally, the cream is whipped unsweetened to contrast the espresso's natural bitterness. Using a whisk or an electric mixer, whip the cream until it forms soft peaks. Be careful not to over-whip; the cream should be thick enough to hold its shape but still soft and spoonable.

3. Assemble the Espresso Con Panna: Carefully spoon or pipe the whipped cream on top of the hot espresso. The cream should sit nicely on top of the espresso, creating a distinct layer. The amount of cream can vary according to personal preference. Typically, the cream layer is about as thick as the espresso layer.

4. Garnish and Serve: For an added touch of elegance, sprinkle a small amount of cocoa powder or chocolate shavings on top of the whipped cream. Serve the Espresso Con Panna immediately. It's recommended to enjoy the drink by stirring the cream into the espresso, blending the two components for a creamy, rich coffee experience.

6.2 Sharing the Joy for Entertaining Friends and Family

75 MULLED COFFEE

A warm, spiced beverage that's perfect for chilly days or festive evenings. It combines the rich, robust flavors of coffee with aromatic spices and a hint of sweetness. This beverage is a wonderful twist on traditional mulled wine and is ideal for coffee lovers seeking something cozy and comforting.

Ingredients:

- » 4 cups of freshly brewed coffee
- » Orange peel: from 1 orange
- » 2 cinnamon sticks
- » 6-8 whole cloves
- » 2 star anise
- » ¼ teaspoon of ground nutmeg
- » 2-3 tablespoons of brown sugar or honey (adjust to taste)
- » 4 ounces of dark rum or brandy (optional)
- » Whipped cream (optional, for topping)
- » Additional cinnamon sticks or orange slices (optional, for garnish)

Preparation Time:
25 minutes

Directions:

1. Brew the Coffee: Start by brewing your coffee. Choose a medium or dark roast for a richer flavor. You can use a drip coffee maker, French press, or any brewing method you prefer.
2. Prepare the Spices: Peel an orange to get long strips of peel, avoiding the white pith as much as possible as it can add bitterness. Gather your cinnamon sticks, whole cloves, star anise, and ground nutmeg.
3. Simmer the Spices: In a large pot, combine the orange peel, cinnamon sticks, cloves, star anise, and nutmeg. Pour the freshly brewed coffee over the spices. Add brown sugar or honey to the pot. Stir well to ensure the sugar or honey dissolves completely. Bring the mixture to a gentle simmer over low heat. Avoid boiling to prevent bitterness. Let it simmer for about 10-15 minutes to allow the flavors to infuse.
4. Add Alcohol (Optional): If using, add dark rum or brandy to the pot. Stir well to combine. This step is optional but can add a lovely warmth and depth to the mulled coffee.
5. Serve: After simmering, strain the coffee to remove the spices and orange peel. Serve the mulled coffee in mugs or heatproof glasses. If desired, top each serving with a dollop of whipped cream. Garnish with a cinnamon stick or an orange slice for an extra festive touch.
6. Enjoy your Mulled Coffee while it's warm. It's a delightful beverage that warms you from the inside out, perfect for sipping on a cold evening or serving at a holiday gathering.

76 COCONUT CREAM COFFEE FOR A CROWD

Coconut Cream Coffee is a pleasant beverage that combines the rich taste of coffee with the exotic flavor of coconut. This recipe is designed for serving a large group, making it perfect for gatherings, brunches, or office meetings. It's a sweet and creamy coffee variation that's sure to impress your guests or colleagues.

Ingredients:

» 8 cups of freshly brewed coffee
» 2 cups of coconut cream
» 1 cup of sweetened condensed milk
» 2 teaspoons of vanilla extract
» 1 teaspoon of ground cinnamon
» For garnish: shredded coconut (toasted, optional)
» Whipped cream (optional): for topping

Preparation Time:
23 minutes

Directions:

1. Brew the Coffee: Start by brewing 8 cups of coffee. Use a quality medium or dark roast to ensure a robust flavor. A large drip coffee maker is ideal for this quantity.
2. Heat the Coconut Cream: In a saucepan, gently heat the coconut cream over low to medium heat. Stir occasionally to prevent it from sticking to the bottom of the pan.
3. Combine Coffee and Coconut Cream: Once the coconut cream is heated (it should be warm but not boiling), pour it into a large coffee urn or a heat-resistant serving dispenser. Add the freshly brewed coffee to the dispenser and stir to combine with the coconut cream.
4. Add Sweetness and Flavor: Stir in the sweetened condensed milk and vanilla extract. These ingredients add sweetness and depth to the coffee. Add ground cinnamon and mix thoroughly. The cinnamon will add a subtle spiciness and warmth to the coffee.
5. Garnish and Serve: If serving immediately, ladle the coffee into individual cups. Top each cup with a dollop of whipped cream and a sprinkle of toasted shredded coconut for an extra touch of luxury and flavor. Alternatively, set up a self-serve station with the coffee dispenser, whipped cream, and shredded coconut for guests to help themselves.
6. Enjoy: Serve the Coconut Cream Coffee warm. It's a comforting and indulgent drink that combines the richness of coffee with the creamy, tropical taste of coconut.

77 ICED CARAMEL MACCHIATO STATION

An Iced Caramel Macchiato Station is a pleasant setup for gatherings or events where guests can enjoy a refreshing and sweet coffee treat. This self-serve station allows everyone to customize their own iced caramel macchiato to their liking.

Ingredients:

» Freshly brewed espresso cooled: about 2-3 shots per serving
» Cold milk or milk alternatives (such as almond, soy, or oat milk): about 1 cup per serving
» 2 tablespoons per serving of vanilla syrup
» For drizzling: Caramel sauce
» Ice cubes
» For topping: whipped cream (optional)
» Additional toppings: chocolate shavings, cinnamon powder, or more caramel sauce

Preparation Time:
20-30 minutes
(depending on the number of servings and setup)

Directions:

1. Prepare the Coffee: Brew enough espresso or strong coffee for the number of expected servings. Allow it to cool to room temperature, then refrigerate to chill it. Using an espresso machine or a strong drip coffee will work well.

2. Set Up the Station: Arrange a table or a designated area with all the necessary ingredients and utensils. Include clear instructions or labels for each ingredient for ease of use. Place the chilled espresso or coffee in a large, easy-to-use dispenser. Organize milk or milk alternatives in pitchers or containers. If offering various types of milk, label them clearly. Set out bottles of vanilla syrup and caramel sauce. Consider using squeeze bottles for easy drizzling. Have a bucket or cooler filled with ice cubes and a scoop. Provide cups, spoons, straws, and napkins for serving.

3. Assembling the Iced Caramel Macchiato: Instruct guests to fill their cup with ice cubes first. Next, they should add vanilla syrup to the ice. Then, add the cold milk to the cup, filling it about three-quarters of the way. Slowly pour the chilled espresso or coffee over the milk. The espresso should create a marbled effect with the milk. Top with a generous drizzle of caramel sauce. For an extra indulgence, whipped cream and additional toppings like chocolate shavings or cinnamon can be added.

4. Enjoy: Guests can stir their Iced Caramel Macchiato to mix the flavors or sip it as is to enjoy the layered taste.

78 CHOCOLATE ESPRESSO MARTINI BAR

An elegant and sophisticated addition to any party or gathering, offering guests the opportunity to indulge in a rich and decadent cocktail. This self-service bar allows everyone to customize their own martini to their liking, mixing the bold flavors of espresso with the sweet indulgence of chocolate.

Ingredients:

For Espresso Martini

» Freshly brewed espresso or strong coffee cooled: about 1 shot per serving
» 1.5 ounces per serving of vodka
» 1 ounce per serving of coffee liqueur (like Kahlúa)
» 1 ounce per serving of chocolate liqueur
» 1/2 ounce per serving of crème de cacao (dark or white)
» Ice cubes
» **For the Bar:** Chocolate syrup: for rimming glasses and drizzling
» Cocoa powder and powdered sugar: for rimming glasses
» Chocolate shavings or chocolate chips: for garnish
» Whipped cream: for topping
» Assorted syrups (like caramel or hazelnut): for additional flavoring
» Shakers, strainers, martini glasses, and measuring jiggers

Preparation Time:
30 minutes (setup and preparation)

Directions:

1. Prepare the Espresso/Coffee: Brew enough espresso or strong coffee for the expected number of servings. Allow it to cool to room temperature and then refrigerate to chill it.

2. Set Up the Martini Bar: Choose a large table or bar area for the setup. Provide clear instructions or labels for each ingredient and tool for ease of use. Organize the vodka, coffee liqueur, chocolate liqueur, and crème de cacao on the bar. Use ice buckets to keep the liqueurs chilled if necessary. Set out the chocolate syrup, cocoa powder, and powdered sugar in separate bowls for rimming the glasses. Arrange the chocolate shavings, chocolate chips, and whipped cream in bowls or dispensers for garnishing the martinis. Include a variety of syrups for guests who want to add extra flavors to their martinis. Ensure there are enough shakers, strainers, martini glasses, and measuring jiggers for guests to use.

3. Assembling the Chocolate Espresso Martini: Guests start by rimming their martini glasses with chocolate syrup, then dipping them into cocoa powder or powdered sugar for an elegant touch. In a shaker, they combine vodka, coffee liqueur, chocolate liqueur, crème de cacao, and chilled espresso or coffee. Add ice to the shaker and instruct them to shake the mixture vigorously until well-chilled. Strain the cocktail into the prepared martini glass. Guests can then garnish their martini with whipped cream, chocolate shavings, or chocolate chips, and drizzle with syrups of their choice.

4. Enjoy: Guests can now enjoy their personalized Chocolate Espresso Martinis, a perfect blend of coffee, chocolate, and vodka.

79 COFFEE SANGRIA

Coffee Sangria is an innovative and delightful twist on the traditional Spanish sangria, combining the rich, bold flavors of coffee with the fruity and refreshing characteristics of classic sangria. This unique beverage is perfect for brunches, gatherings, or as an intriguing addition to your cocktail menu.

Ingredients:

Preparation Time:
15 minutes
(plus chilling time,
preferably 2-4 hours)

» 3 cups of freshly brewed coffee cooled to room temperature
» 1 bottle - Brandy or rum: ½ cup of red wine (preferably a fruity one like Tempranillo or Grenache)
» ¼ cup of orange liqueur (like Triple Sec or Cointreau)
» ¼ cup of simple syrup adjust to taste
» 2 oranges sliced
» 1 lemon sliced
» 1 Apple cored and sliced
» 1 cup of berries (like strawberries or raspberries)
» Sparkling water or club soda: to top up (optional)
» Ice cubes

Directions:

1. Brew and Cool the Coffee: Start by brewing your coffee. You can use any brewing method you prefer. Once brewed, allow the coffee to cool to room temperature.
2. Prepare the Fruit: Wash and slice the oranges and lemons into thin rounds. Core and slice the apple. If using strawberries, hull and halve them. Raspberries can be used whole.
3. Mix the Sangria: In a large pitcher, combine the cooled coffee, red wine, brandy or rum, and orange liqueur. Add the simple syrup to the mixture. You can adjust the amount of syrup depending on how sweet you like your sangria. Stir well to ensure all the ingredients are thoroughly mixed.
4. Add the Fruit: Add the sliced oranges, lemons, apples, and berries to the pitcher. Stir gently to mix the fruit with the liquid.
5. Chill the Sangria: Cover the pitcher and refrigerate for at least 2 to 4 hours, ideally overnight. This allows the flavors to meld and the fruit to infuse the sangria.
6. Serve: To serve, fill glasses with ice cubes and pour the sangria over them, making sure to get some fruit pieces in each glass. If desired, top up each glass with a splash of sparkling water or club soda for a refreshing fizz. Garnish with additional fruit slices or berries if desired.
7. Enjoy: Enjoy your Coffee Sangria chilled. It's a perfect balance of coffee's depth with the fruity and vibrant flavors of traditional sangria.

80 PEPPERMINT COFFEE BLISS

Peppermint Coffee Bliss is a refreshing and indulgent beverage that combines the invigorating taste of coffee with the cool and minty flavor of peppermint. This drink is perfect for those who enjoy a minty twist to their coffee, making it an ideal choice for a festive treat or a cozy pick-me-up.

Ingredients:

» 2 cups of freshly brewed hot coffee
» 2-3 tablespoons of peppermint syrup (adjust to taste)
» ½ cup of milk or a milk alternative
» For topping: whipped cream
» For garnish: Crushed peppermint candies or candy canes
» For garnish: Chocolate shavings or cocoa powder
» Ice cubes (optional, for an iced version)

Preparation Time:
10 minutes

Directions:

1. Brew the Coffee: Start by brewing your favorite coffee. A medium or dark roast works well for this recipe, as it complements the peppermint flavor.
2. Prepare the Peppermint Coffee: In each coffee cup, pour 1 to 1.5 tablespoons of peppermint syrup. Adjust the amount based on how strong you prefer the peppermint flavor. Pour the hot brewed coffee over the syrup in each cup. Stir well to ensure the syrup is fully mixed with the coffee.
3. Heat and Froth the Milk (Optional): If you prefer a creamier texture, heat the milk in a saucepan or use a milk frother to warm and froth the milk. Gently pour the heated or frothed milk into the coffee, stirring lightly.
4. Add Whipped Cream: Top each cup of coffee with a generous dollop of whipped cream. This adds a rich and creamy texture to the drink.
5. Garnish: Sprinkle crushed peppermint candies or candy cane pieces over the whipped cream. This not only adds a festive look but also enhances the minty flavor. For an added touch of indulgence, sprinkle chocolate shavings or a dusting of cocoa powder on top.
6. Serve and Enjoy: Serve the Peppermint Coffee Bliss immediately. Enjoy the warming and comforting flavors of coffee and peppermint in each sip.
7. For an Iced Version: To make an iced version of Peppermint Coffee Bliss, fill a glass with ice cubes before adding the peppermint syrup and coffee. Then, top with cold milk, whipped cream, and garnishes.

THE COFFEE LIFE STYLE

In the modern lexicon of our daily lives, coffee emerges not merely as a beverage but as a cultural phenomenon, a ritual infused with an ethos that transcends its physical form. This chapter seeks to unravel the tapestry of the coffee lifestyle, exploring its capacity to embed itself as a pivotal element in our daily routines, augment mindfulness, and cultivate a sense of community.

7.1 Cultivating a Coffee Ritual: Integrating Coffee into Daily Existence

The practice of consuming coffee extends beyond mere habituation; it ascends to the realm of ritual, setting the tenor for the day's proceedings. Thoughtful incorporation of coffee into one's daily life amplifies its intrinsic pleasure and accentuates its benefits. To this end, a compendium of suggestions is presented:

Morning Coffee Ceremony: Inaugurate a daily coffee-making ceremony. This could range from the grinding of fresh beans to the meticulous preparation of a pour-over, transforming this process into a treasured element of your morning routine.

Coffee Chronicle Keeping: Maintain a journal dedicated to your coffee experiences. Document the variety of coffees sampled, the methods of brewing employed, and your personal reflections. This discipline serves to deepen your appreciation and insight into the world of coffee.

Knowledge and Experimentation: Engage regularly in the study of diverse coffee cultures, beans, and brewing techniques. Venture into novel brewing methods and flavors, thus infusing your routine with a sense of excitement and discovery.

Meditative Brewing: Treat the act of coffee preparation as a meditative exercise. Concentrate on the procedure, savor the aromas, and relish the flavors, anchoring yourself in the present.

Social Coffee Interludes: Weave coffee into your social fabric, whether it be a coffee rendezvous with a friend or a morning coffee gathering in a professional setting. These instances can forge and fortify relationships, enriching your social life.

7.2 Coffee and Mindfulness: Savoring Coffee with Conscious Presence

Imbibing coffee can evolve into a practice of mindfulness, elevating it from a simple routine to a profoundly enriching experience. Here's how one might engage in this mindful practice:

Moment of Appreciation: Before indulging in the first sip, pause to acknowledge the aroma. Allow this olfactory experience to anchor you in the immediacy of the present.

Sensory Engagement: As you partake in your coffee, attune yourself to its taste, warmth, and texture. Observe the subtle shifts in its character as it gradually cools.

Reflective Coffee Time: Utilize your coffee interlude for introspection. It could serve as a juncture for planning your day, indulging in creative thought, or engaging in tranquil reverie.

Practice of Gratitude: Cultivate a habit of gratitude towards your coffee. Contemplate its journey from bean to cup and the multitude of hands that facilitated its passage.

Periods of Tranquility: Designate your coffee breaks as intervals free from technological intrusion. Utilize these moments to detach from the digital sphere and reconnect with your inner self.

7.3 Coffee Connections: Nurturing Community Through Coffee

Coffee possesses an intrinsic ability to connect individuals, fostering communal bonds and shared experiences. Here are various avenues through which this community-building aspect of coffee can be nurtured:

Coffee Tastings and Socials: Initiate or participate in coffee-tasting sessions and social gatherings. These could be informal domestic settings or structured events at local coffee establishments.

Coffee Clubs: Join or establish a coffee club, a conclave where aficionados can exchange their preferred beans, recipes, and experiences.

Participation in Coffee Workshops: Enroll in workshops or classes that delve into various facets of coffee. These platforms are splendid venues for encountering fellow coffee enthusiasts.

Patronage of Local Coffee Establishments: Regular visits to neighborhood coffee shops can integrate you into the local coffee community. Engage with baristas and fellow patrons, sharing stories and recommendations.

In essence, coffee is more than a mere beverage; it is a medium for connection, a catalyst for mindfulness, and an integral component of our daily rituals. Embracing the coffee lifestyle opens doors to a richer, more interconnected existence. Let it not just be a part of your life, but a facilitator of moments, experiences, and relationships.

COFFEE GLOSSARY

Terms Every Coffee Lover Should Know

In the realm of coffee connoisseurship, a myriad of terms defines the experience. From the subtle nuances of taste to the intricate methods of preparation, each term offers insight into the rich tapestry of coffee culture.

Acidity: This term describes a pleasant tartness in coffee, often perceived as a brightness when mild, and increasingly sharp as intensity grows.

Affogato: Hailing from Italy, this dessert coffee combines vanilla gelato or ice cream with a hot espresso pour-over, creating a delightful fusion.

Arabica: Indigenous to Yemen's mountains, Arabica is a coffee species renowned for its superior quality over its counterpart, Robusta.

Barista: Skilled artisans of the coffee world, baristas expertly prepare and serve a range of coffee drinks, typically within the confines of a café.

Blend: A harmonious amalgamation of beans from various locales, bean types, or roasting levels, blended coffees offer complex flavor profiles.

Bourbon: A variant of Arabica, noted for its intricate acidity and well-balanced flavor.

Crema: Characteristic of freshly brewed espresso, crema is the creamy, tan foam that adorns the top.

Cupping: A standardized technique employed to assess coffee beans' aroma and flavor nuances.

Decaffeination: The art of caffeine extraction from coffee beans, retaining flavor while reducing stimulant content.

Espresso: A potent coffee brew, Espresso is a strong coffee made by forcing hot water through finely ground beans under pressure.

French Press: A brewing device where hot water and coffee grounds meet, separated by a plunger's press.

Grinder: An essential tool in coffee preparation, grinders transform beans into the grounds necessary for brewing.

Latte: A blend of espresso and steamed milk that creates a harmonious flavor.

Macchiato: Espresso graced with a touch of foamed milk.

Microfoam: The foundation of latte art, microfoam comprises finely frothed milk with a velvety texture.

Mocha: A delectable mix of chocolate syrup, espresso, steamed milk, often crowned with whipped cream.

Organic Coffee: Grown without synthetic fertilizers or pesticides, organic coffee is a nod to natural cultivation methods.

Pour-Over: A brewing technique involving the meticulous pouring of water over grounds in a filter, leading to a deliberate drip into a carafe or mug.

Robusta: A robust coffee species known for its high caffeine content and bitter taste, in contrast to Arabica. Single-origin coffee can be traced back to a specific producer, crop, or region within a country.

Single-Origin: Coffee that traces its lineage to a single producer, crop, or region within one country.

Third Wave Coffee: Part of a movement that views coffee as an artisanal foodstuff akin to wine, focusing on high-quality production and appreciation.

Turkish Coffee: A traditional preparation method involving boiling finely ground coffee with sugar (and sometimes cardamom), served in a cup where grounds settle naturally.

Wet Processing: A method that involves removing pulp and skin from coffee cherries using water before drying, yielding a cleaner, more acidic bean.

This compendium of coffee terminology not only serves as an educational tool for enthusiasts but also enriches the dialogue within the coffee community, allowing for a more nuanced and informed appreciation of this beloved beverage."

SPECIAL THANKS

As the completion of this coffee-centric journey comes to fruition, it's important to pause and express gratitude to everyone who contributed to the creation and success of this book.

First and foremost, I would like to thank the coffee growers around the world whose tireless efforts and dedication to their craft provide us with the diverse and quality coffee beans that are the foundation of every cup.

A heartfelt thank you to the coffee researchers and scientists who have expanded our knowledge and appreciation for coffee through their studies and findings on its health effects, cultivation methods, and impact on the environment.

To the baristas and coffee shop owners who serve as the day-to-day ambassadors of coffee culture, your passion for coffee and commitment to sharing it with the world does not go unnoticed. Your insights and feedback have been invaluable.

Gratitude is also owed to the many tasters, food stylists, and photographers who brought the recipes in this book to life through their keen senses and artistic talents.

A special thanks to the editors, designers, and publishers for their keen eyes and expertise in shaping this manuscript into something that can sit proudly on any coffee lover's shelf.

To the family and friends who have supported this endeavor, whether by acting as taste testers or providing a listening ear during the writing process, your support has been a source of constant encouragement.

And, of course, to the coffee community at large — from the casual drinkers to the connoisseurs — your enthusiasm for coffee continues to inspire and drive the dialogue around this beloved beverage forward.

Lastly, thank you to you, the reader, for your curiosity and eagerness to delve deeper into the world of coffee. May this book enrich your understanding and enjoyment of coffee, and perhaps even help you discover your new favorite brew.

Without all of you, this book would not have been possible. Thank you.

Warmest regards,

Arabella Bennet

INDEX

Made in the USA
Monee, IL
27 December 2024

75505063R00057